Wingham Ontario and Area in Colour Photos, Saving Our History One Photo at a Time

Photography
by Barbara Raué
2022

Series Name: Cruising Ontario

Book 199: Wingham, Auburn, Belgrave, Blyth, Carlow, Dunlop

Cover photo: 274 Josephine Street, Wingham, Page 9

Series Name: Cruising Ontario
Saving Our History One Photo at a Time
in colour photos

Towns in Alphabetical Order:
Aberfoyle, Acton, Alton, Amherstburg, Ancaster, Arthur, Auburn, Aylmer, Ayr, Beaver Valley, Belgrave, Belleville, Bloomingdale, Blyth, Brantford, Brockville, Burford, Burlington, Caledon, Caledonia, Cambridge, Carlow, Chatsworth, Clifford, Collingwood, Conestogo, Delhi, Dorchester to Aylmer, Drayton, Drumbo, Dundas, Dunlop, Eden Mills, Elmira, Elora, Erin, Essex, Fergus, Goderich, Grimsby, Guelph, Hagersville, Hamilton, Hanover, Harriston, Hespeler, Jarvis, Kingston, Kingsville, Kitchener, Lake Superior, Lincoln, Linwood, Listowel, London, Lucknow, Merrickville, Mono, Mount Forest, Mount Pleasant, Neustadt, New Hamburg, Newboro, Newport, Niagara-on-the-Lake, Oakville, Onondaga, Orangeville, Orillia, Owen Sound, Palmerston, Paris, Pelham, Perth, Peterborough, Petrolia, Port Colborne, Port Elgin, Portland, Preston, Rockwood, Sarnia, Sault Ste. Marie, Seaforth, Sheffield, Shelburne, Simcoe, Smiths Falls, Smithville, Southampton, St. Catharines, St. George, St. Jacobs, St. Marys, St. Thomas, Stoney Creek, Stratford, Thamesford, Thunder Bay, Tillsonburg, Toronto, Waterdown, Waterford, Waterloo, Welland, Wellesley, Westport, Windsor, Wingham, Woodstock

Book 196: Pelham
Book 197: Beaver Valley
Book 198: Chatsworth
Book 199: Wingham

Table of Contents

Wingham	Page 6
Auburn	Page 46
Belgrave	Page 48
Blyth	Page 50
Carlow	Page 62
Dunlop	Page 63
Architectural Terms	Page 64
Building Styles	Page 67

Wingham is located in the municipality of North Huron in Huron County. Wingham became part of North Huron in 2001 when the Ontario government imposed amalgamation on the former township of East Wawanosh, the village of Blyth, and the town of Wingham. Wingham is located where two branches of the Maitland River converge. County Road 86 connects to Kitchener-Waterloo to the east; the main thoroughfare is County Road 4, called Josephine Street within Wingham, and connects to London, Ontario to the south. Wingham became a prominent supply and distribution centre for the agricultural and lumbering hinterland. Railway expansion in the 1870s stimulated further growth. Wingham has three radio stations and a television station.

The Township of Ashfield-Colborne-Wawanosh is a municipality in the northwest corner of Huron County. It was formed as an amalgamation of the former Ashfield, Colborne and West Wawanosh townships in 2001. The three former townships now comprise the wards of the amalgamated municipality. Lake Huron is the western boundary and the Township has more than thirty-five kilometers of Lake Huron shoreline. Its southern boundary is the Maitland River between Goderich and Auburn. The eastern border is Huron Road 22, from Auburn north to Huron Road 86 near Whitechurch. Huron Road 86 is generally the northern border of Ashfield–Colborne–Wawanosh except for the Lucknow community limits which are in Bruce County. The township encompasses the communities of Amberley, Auburn, Benmiller, Carlow, Dungannon, Kingsbridge, Kintail, Nile, Port Albert, St. Augustine, St. Helens and Saltford.

By 1869, Belgrave was a village with a population of 50 in the Township of Morris County, Huron. It was established on the Maitland River. It was a stop on the Buffalo and Lake Huron Railway. There were stages to Wingham Teeswater Riversdale and Kincardine. The average price of land was $20.

By 1851, Lucius McConnell and Kenneth McBain were two of the earliest settlers in Morris Township. Four years later, Donald McDonald laid out a village plot on the border between Wawanosh and Morris Townships and the village of Blyth developed. By 1858, the village had a post office, sawmill, Presbyterian Church, a tavern and a store. A station on the London, Huron and Bruce Railway was opened here in 1876.

Wingham

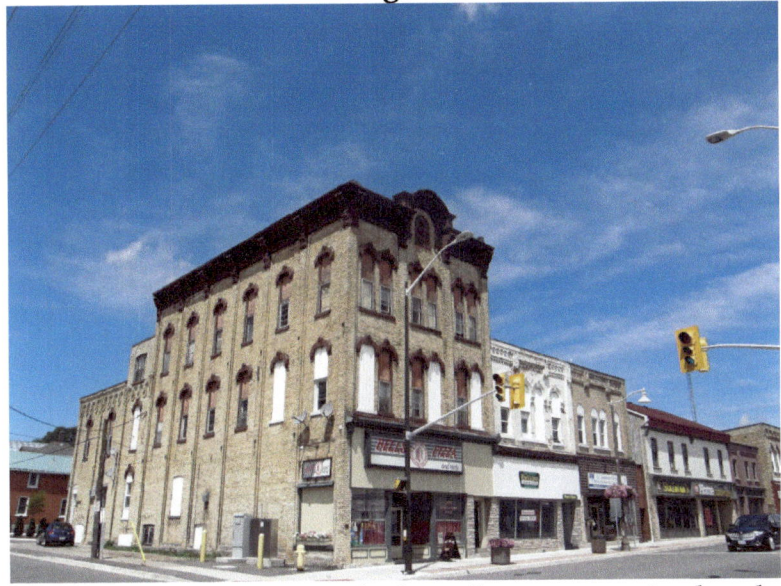

176 Josephine Street - Kent Block – pilasters, cornice brackets, voussoirs, keystones

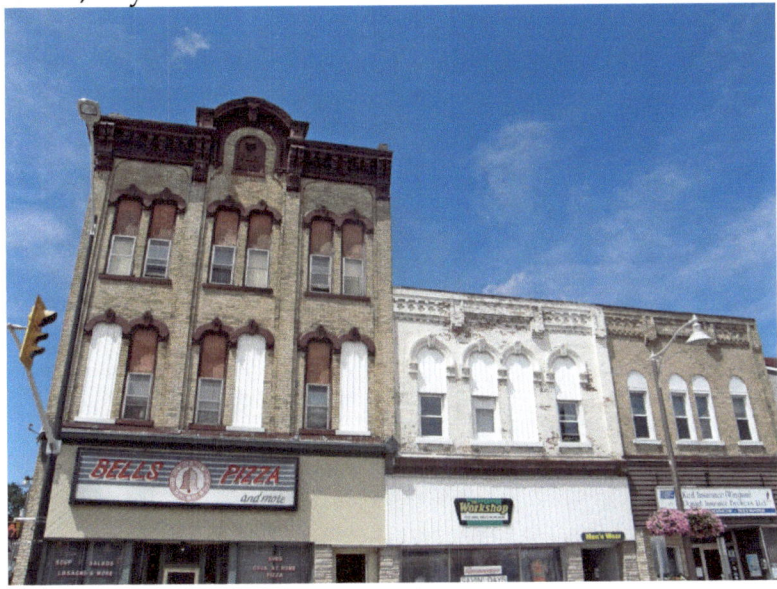

176-180 Josephine Street

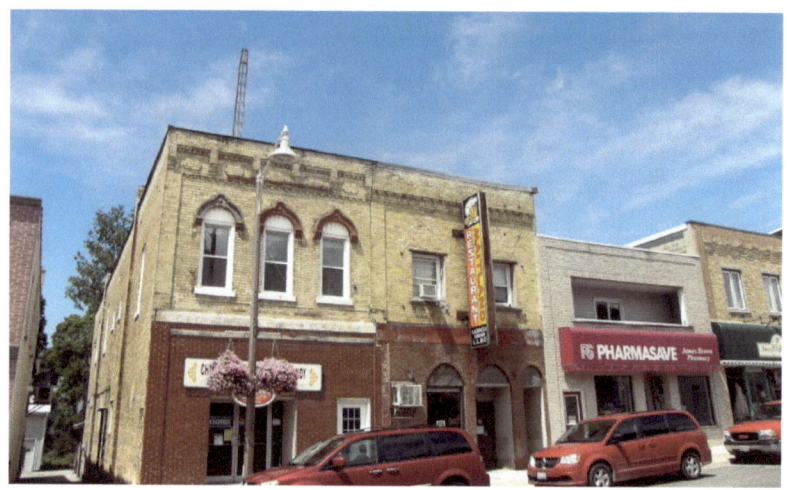

194 Josephine Street – Maitland Restaurant

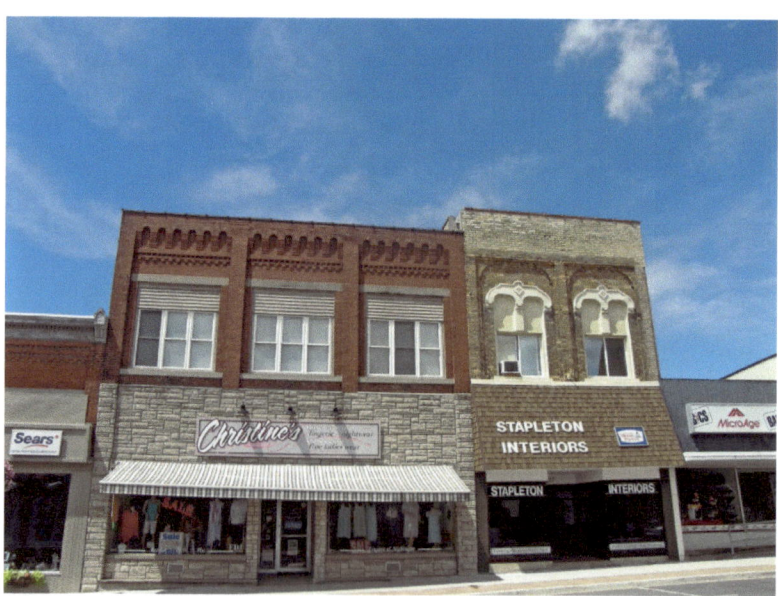

208-212 Josephine Street – Christine's Clothes Closet and Stapleton Interiors

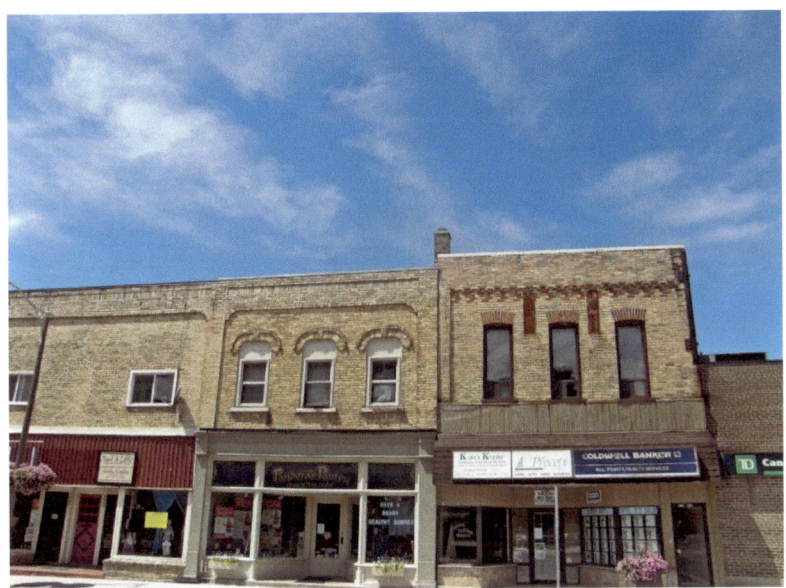
218-224 Josephine Street – Pandora's Pantry

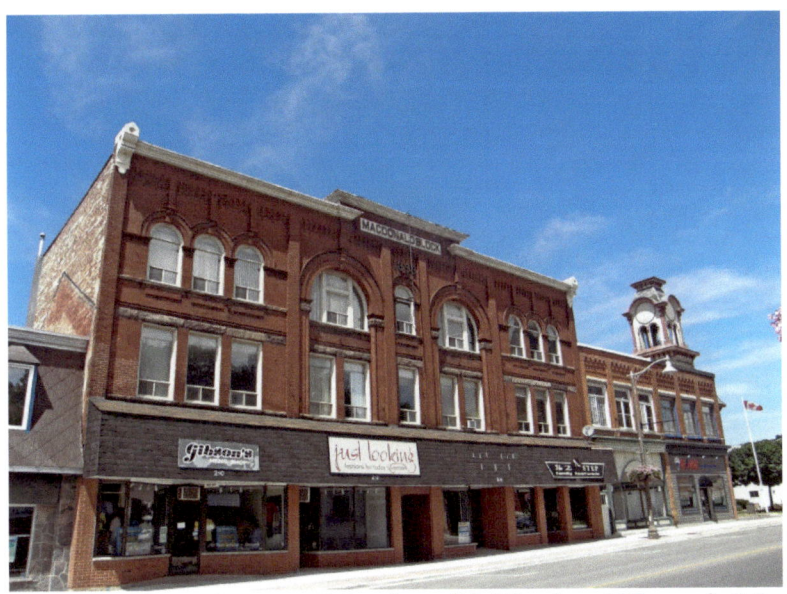
250-256 Josephine Street - Macdonald Block – Gibson's Men's Shop, Just Looking (Women's)

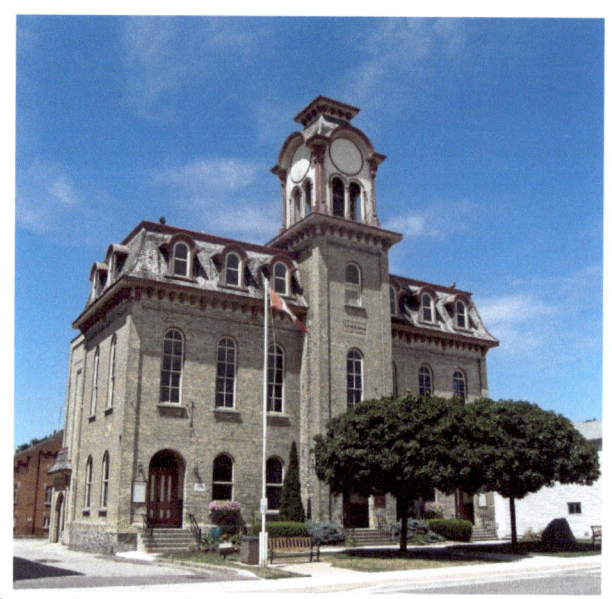

274 Josephine Street - Town Hall – A.D. 1890 – Second Empire style – mansard roof with dormers

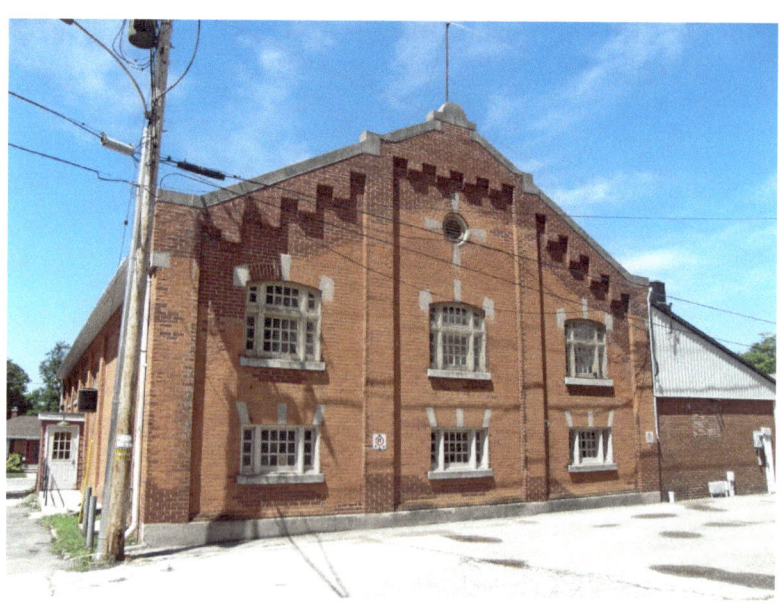

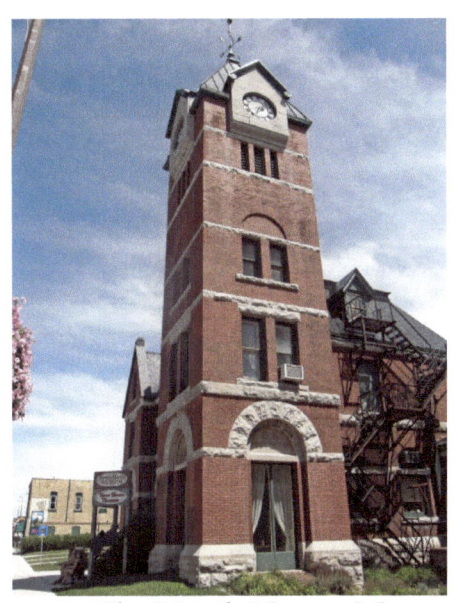

273 Josephine Street - The North Huron Museum celebrates the history of the north Huron area from the Paleolithic era to modern day. It is housed in the former Post Office building which served Wingham and area residents from 1907 to 1968.

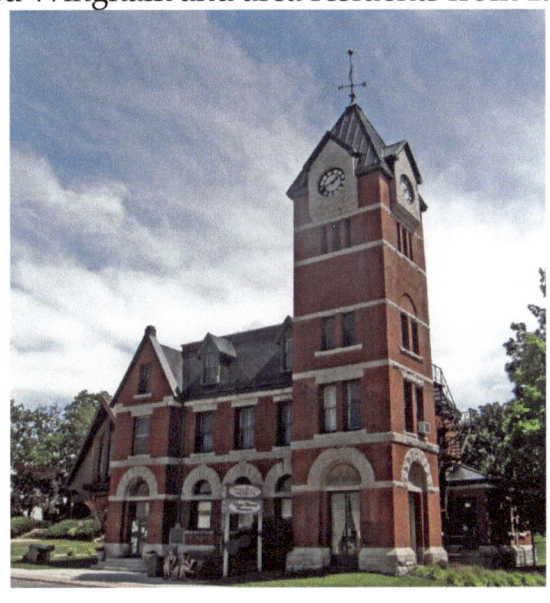

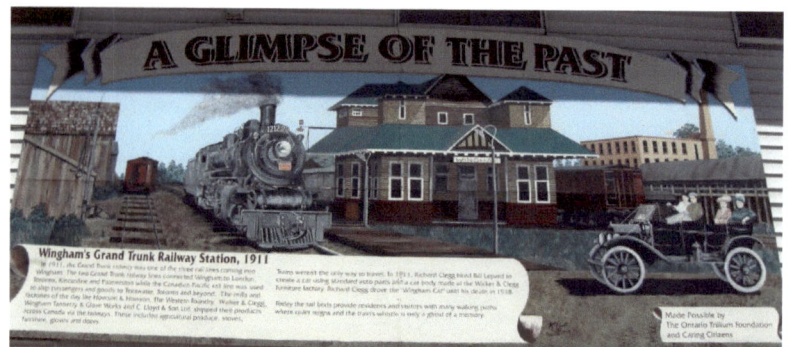

In 1911, Wingham's Grand Trunk Railway Station was one of the three rail lines coming into Wingham. The two Grand Trunk Railway lines connected Wingham to London, Toronto, Kincardine and Palmerston while the Canadian Pacific rail line shipped passengers and goods to Teeswater, Toronto and beyond. Today the rail beds have become walking trails.

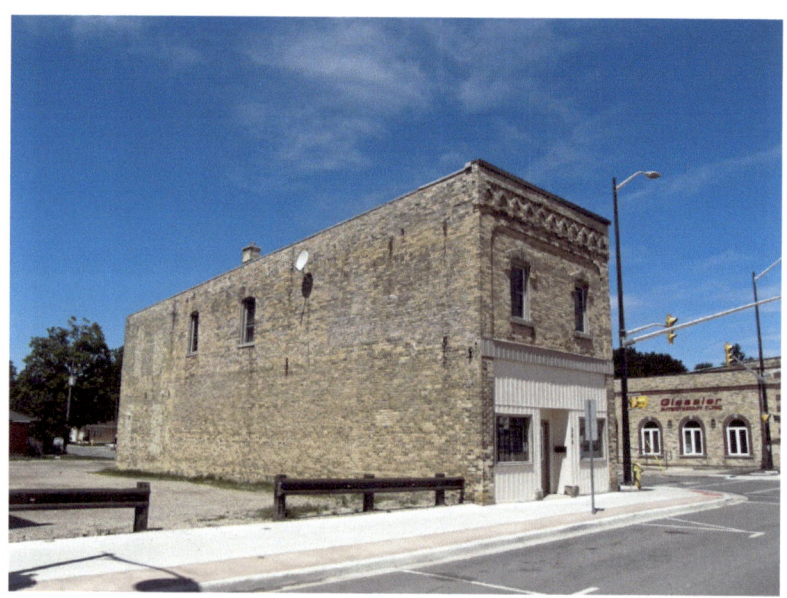

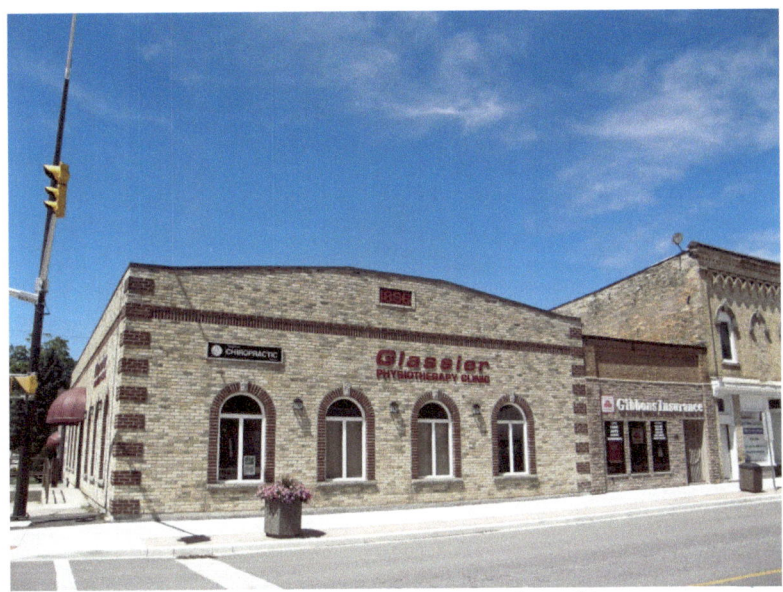

Josephine Street – 1896 - corner quoins, banding, voussoirs and keystones

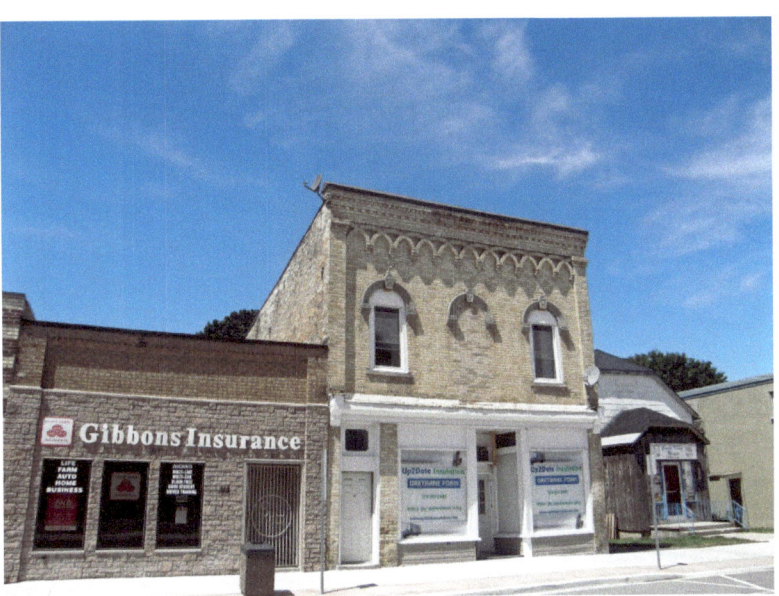

318-320 Josephine Street

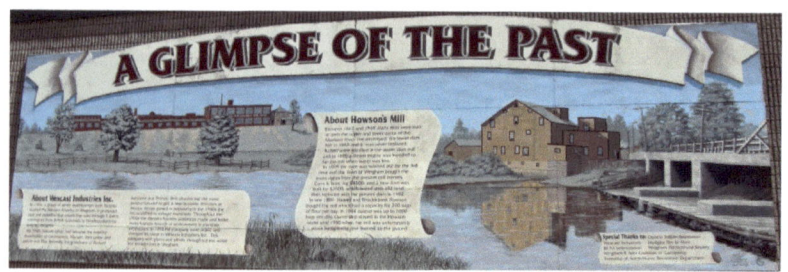

Between 1862 and 1888, many mills were built at both the upper and lower dams on the Maitland River. Fire destroyed the lower dam mill in 1888 and it was never replaced. Rollers were installed in the upper dam mill and in 1895 a steam engine was installed to run the mill when the water was low. In 1899 the dam was washed out for the third time and the Town of Wingham bought the water rights from the mill owners of Carrs and Brothers for $4,000 and a new dam was built for $3,500 which lasted until 1921. The present dam was built in 1982. In late 1899, Harvey and Brocklebank Howson bought the mill which had a capacity of two hundred bags of flour per day. Ownership stayed in the Howson family until 1950 when the mill was struck by lightning and burned to the ground.

In 1902 a group of seven businessmen from Toronto started the Western Foundry in Wingham. It produced coal and wood-burning stoves that sold through T. Eaton catalogues from British Columbia to Newfoundland for more than six decades. By 1960 William LeVan was the majority shareholder of the business. His son, Dick LeVan, and son-in-law, Don Kennedy, the grandsons of Richard Vanstone and Thomas Bell, phased out the stove production and forged a new business direction as electric stoves became popular. In the 1980s the focus shifted to exhaust manifolds. In 1994 the company went public and changed the name to Westcast Industries Inc. This company with plants and offices around the world has strong roots in Wingham.

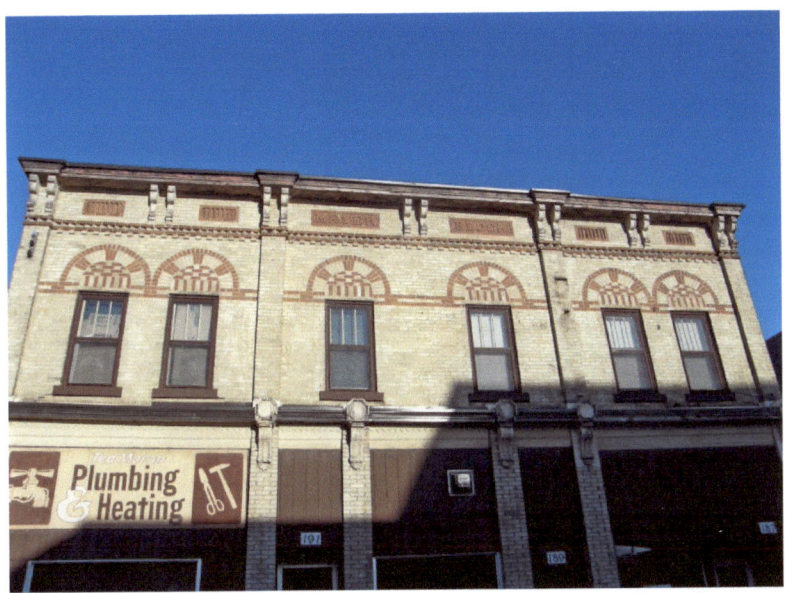

187-193 Josephine Street – dichromatic brickwork, pilasters, cornice brackets

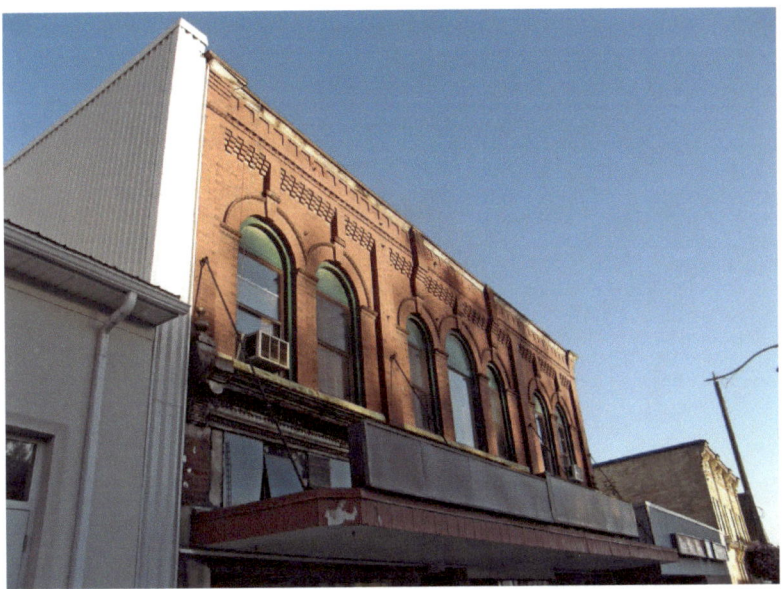

Voussoirs and keystones, pilasters, bevelled dentil molding

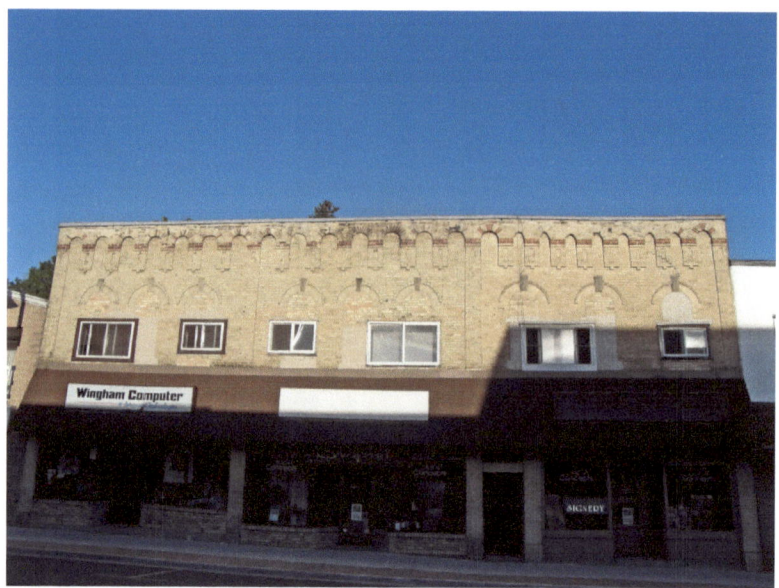

245 Josephine Street – dichromatic brickwork, voussoirs, keystones

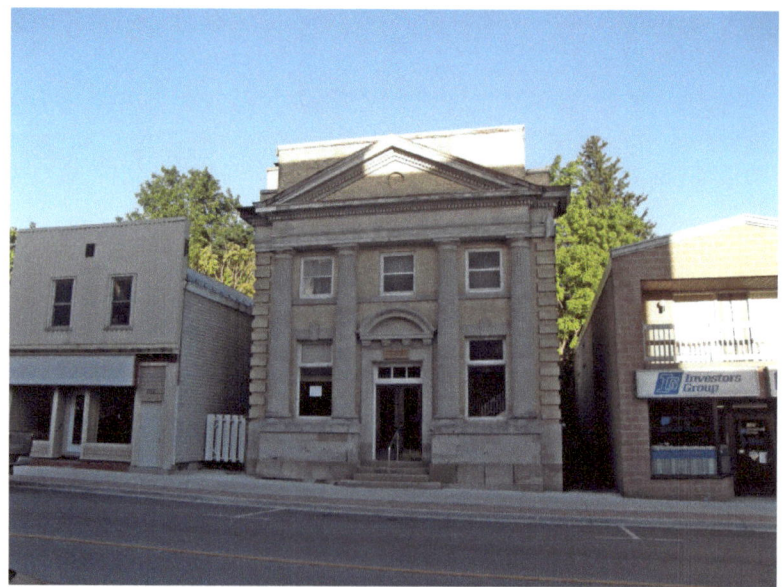

253 Josephine Street - This Neo-Classical building was built in 1907 to house the new Bank of Commerce which operated here from 1907 to 1923.

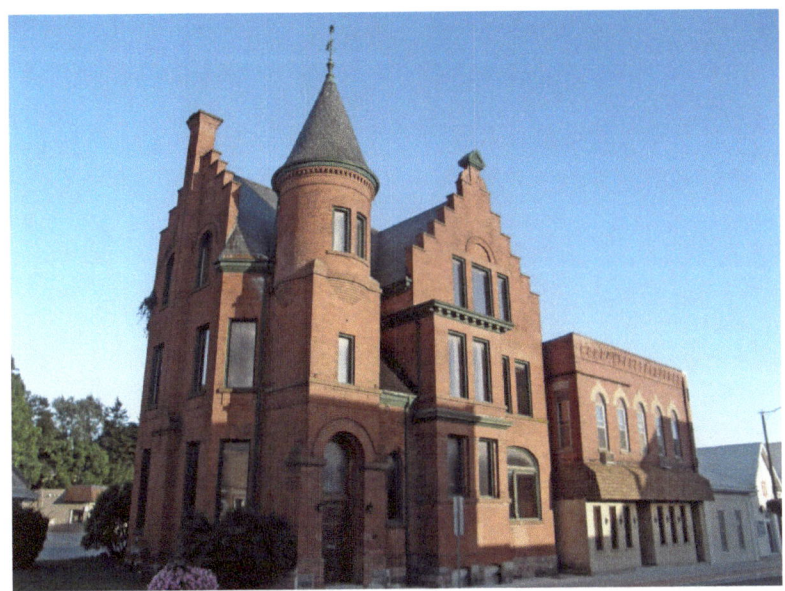

Romanesque – Jacobean gables, three-story tower

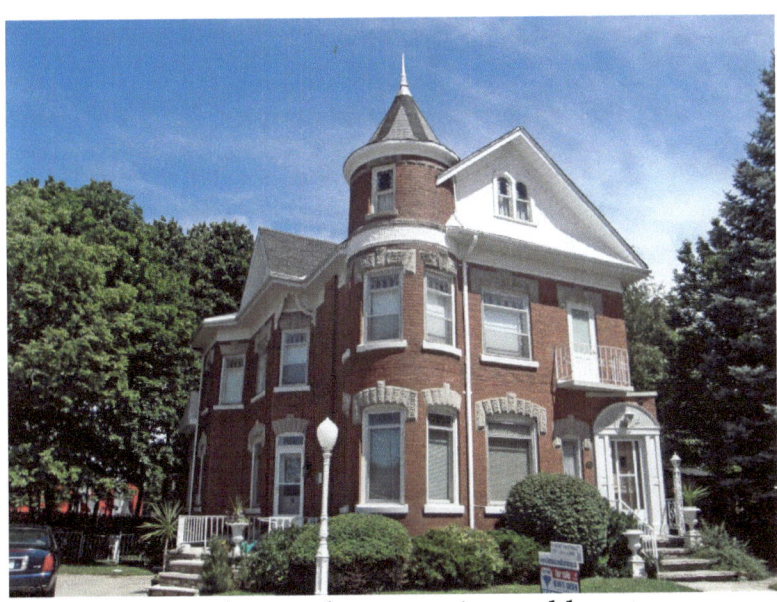

Three-story turret, fretwork, voussoirs and keystones, decorative cornice, second floor balcony

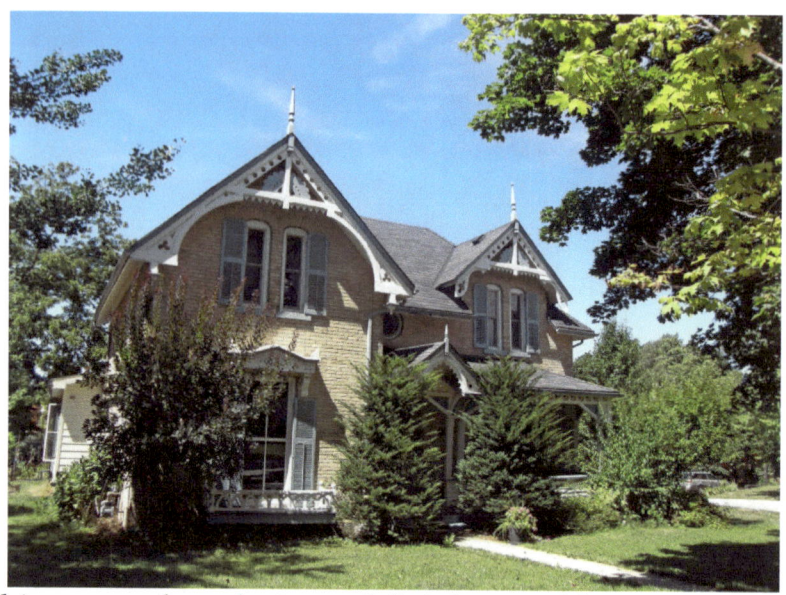
Gothic – verge board trim and finials on gables, window hood above first floor window

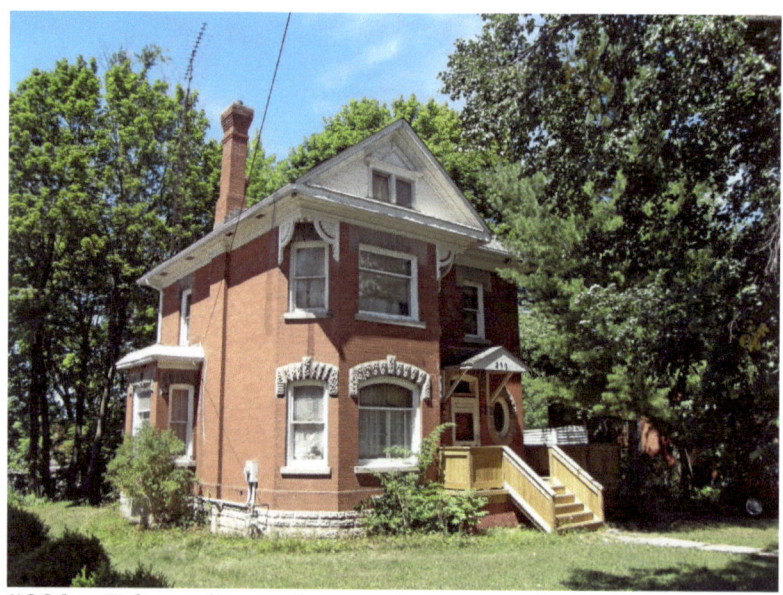
#290 – Edwardian – fretwork, voussoirs and keystones

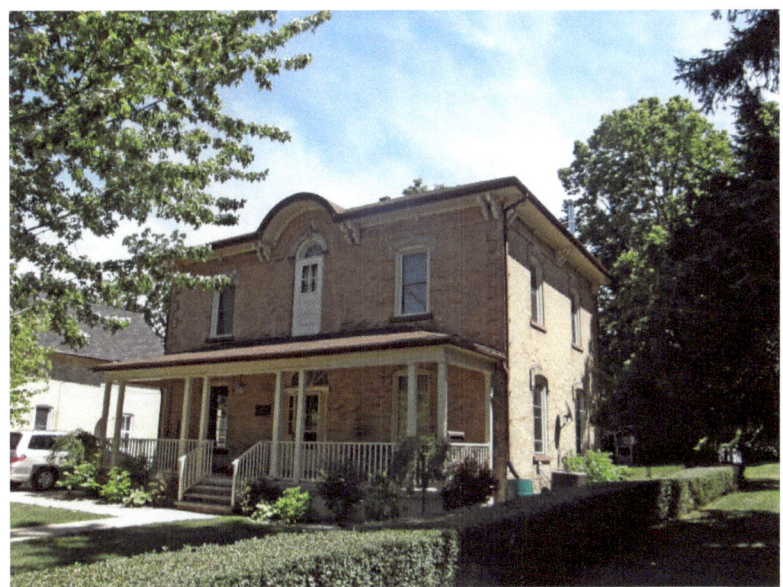

#289 – corner quoins, paired cornice brackets, sidelights and multi-paned transom window surrounding door

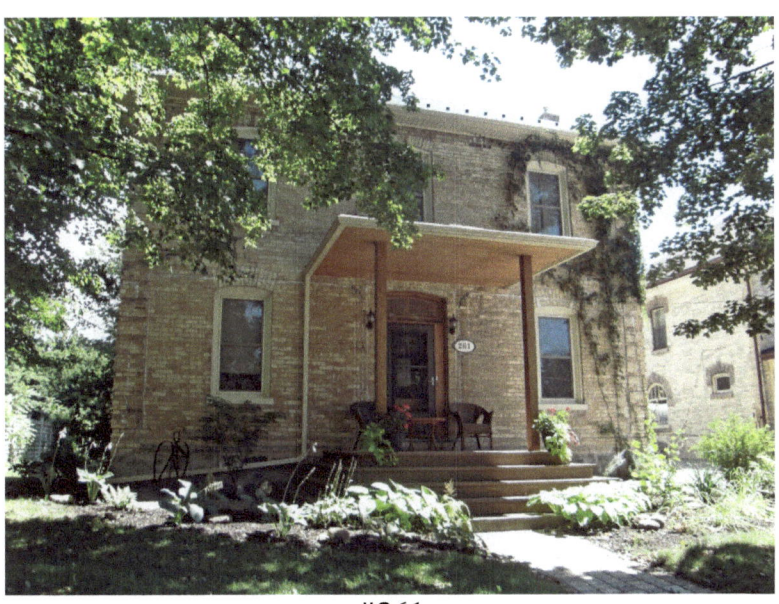

#261

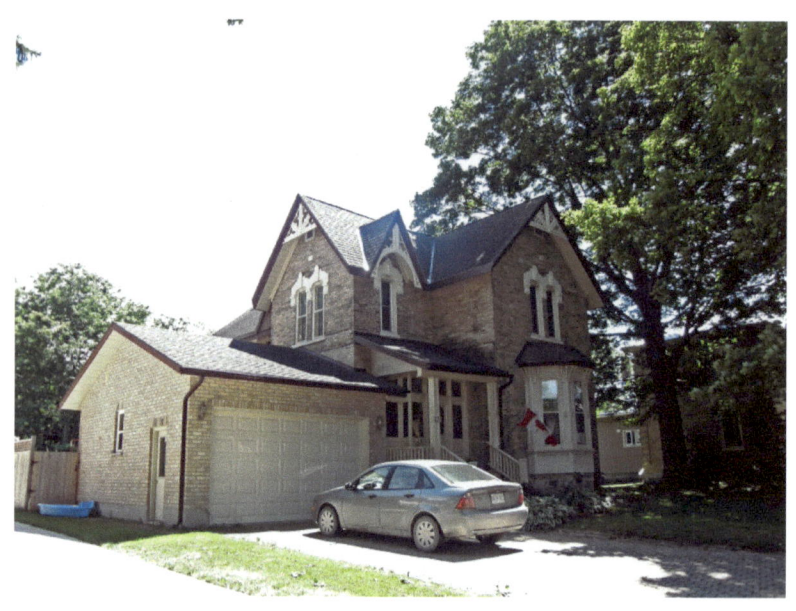

#271 – Gothic – verge board trim on gables, voussoirs and keystones, bay window

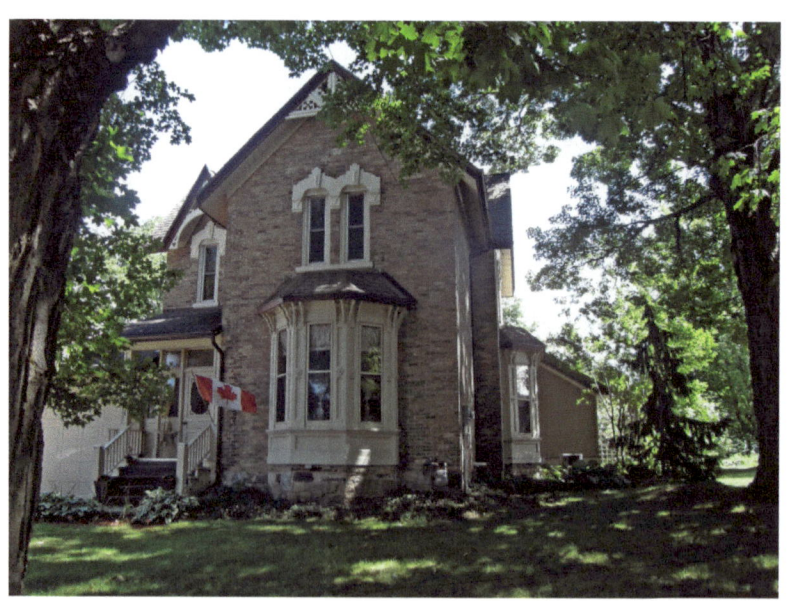

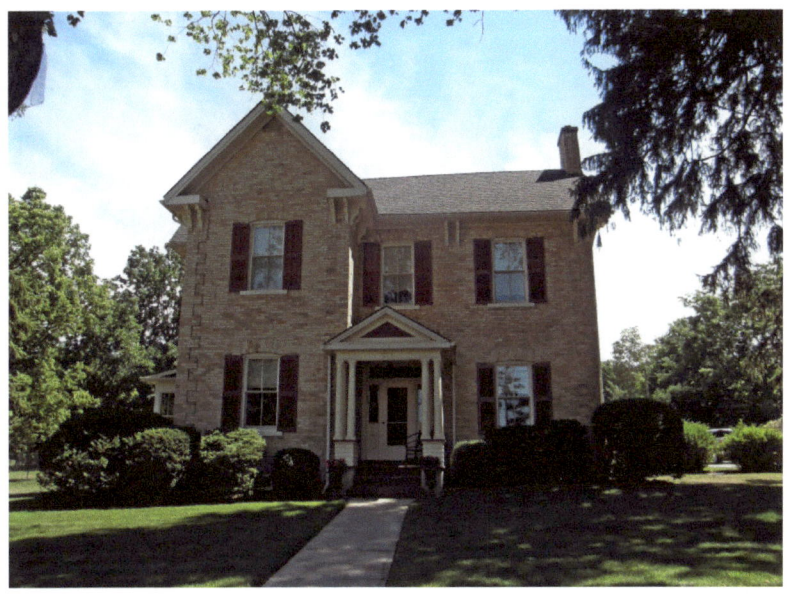

#277 – cornice return on gable, brackets, pediment above Doric pillars, sidelights and transom

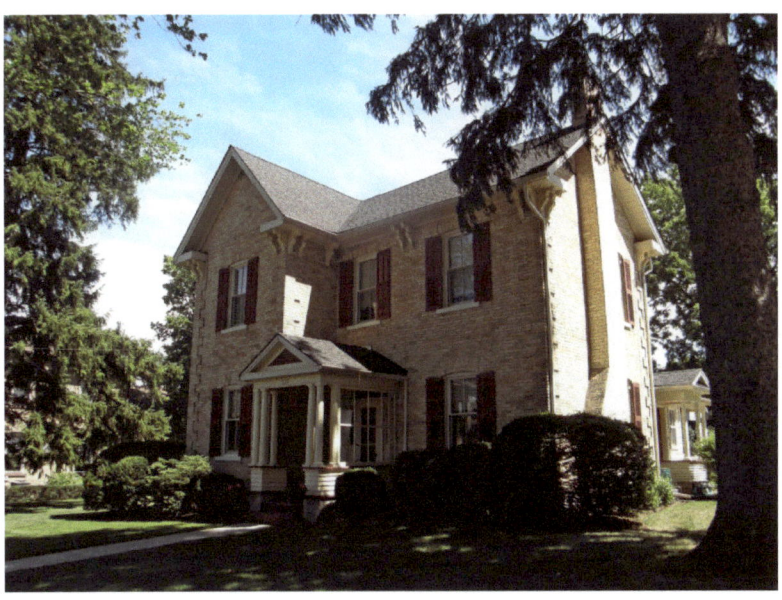

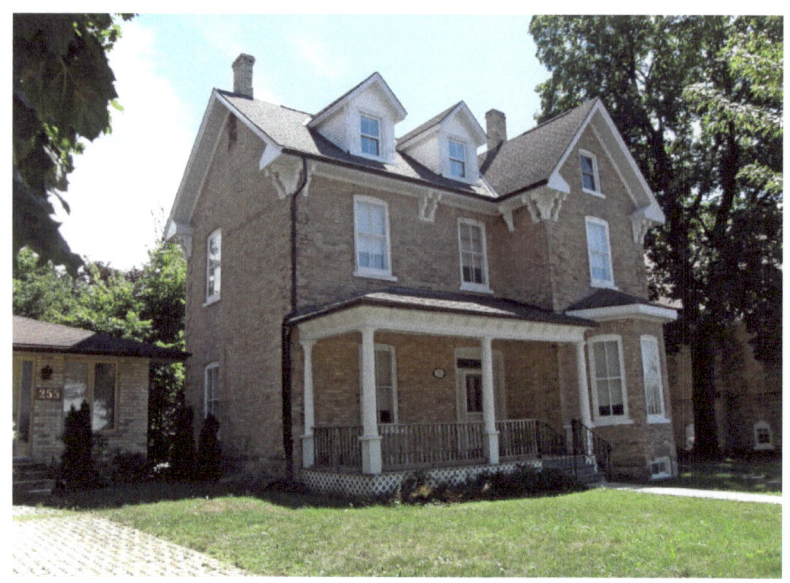

#251 – dormers, cornice brackets, bay window

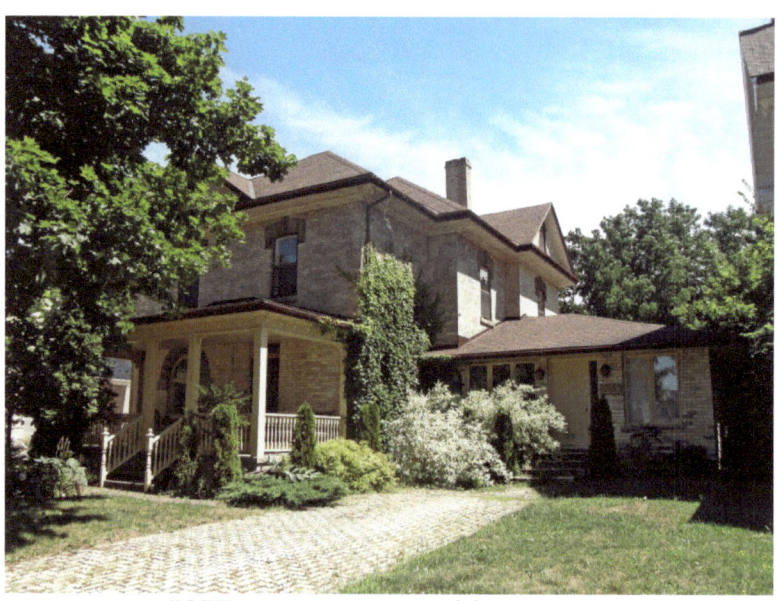

#255 – voussoirs and keystones

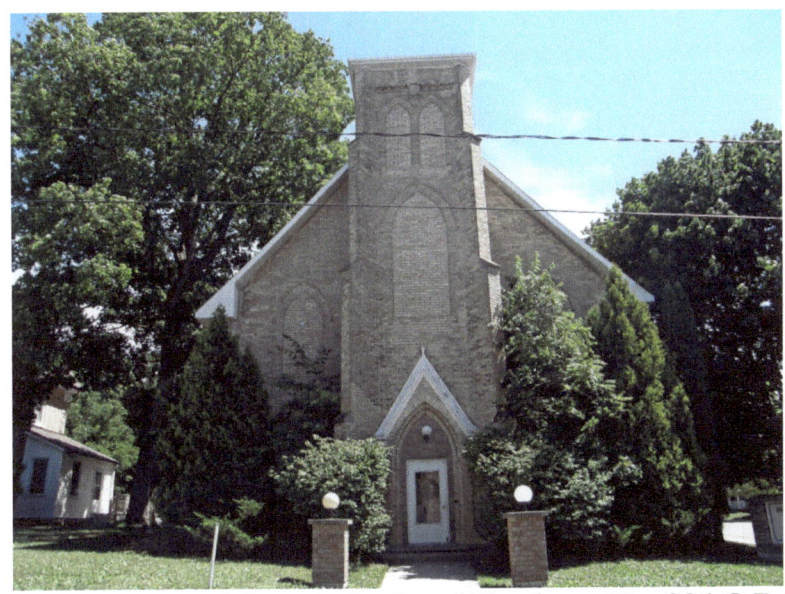

241 Centre Street - Masonic Lodge, Wingham No. 286 G.R.C. - voussoirs

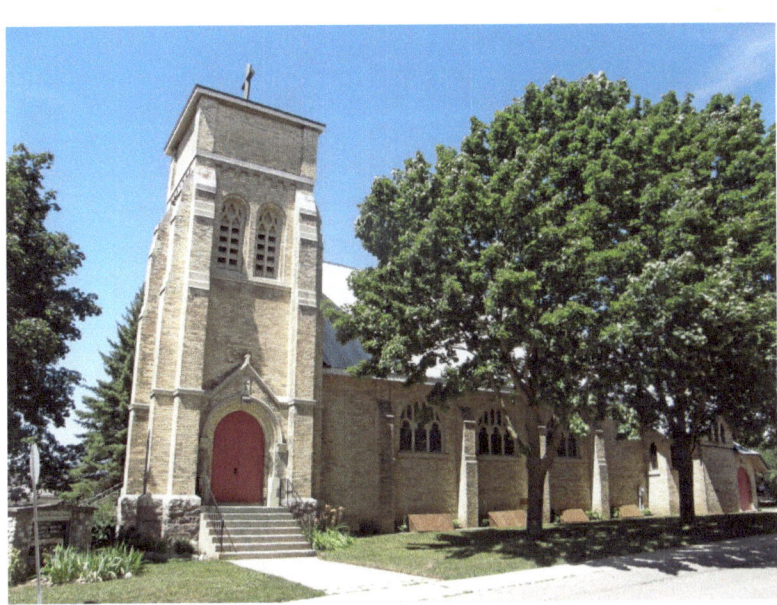

19 John Street East - St. Paul's Trinity Church – buttresses, muntins on windows, dentil molding

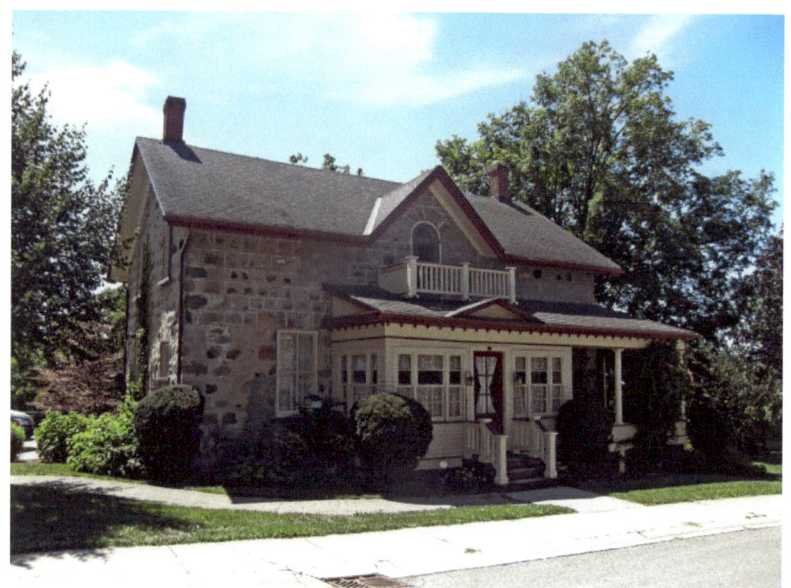

26 John Street East – Gothic style stone building, second floor balcony, pediment with sunburst in tympanum

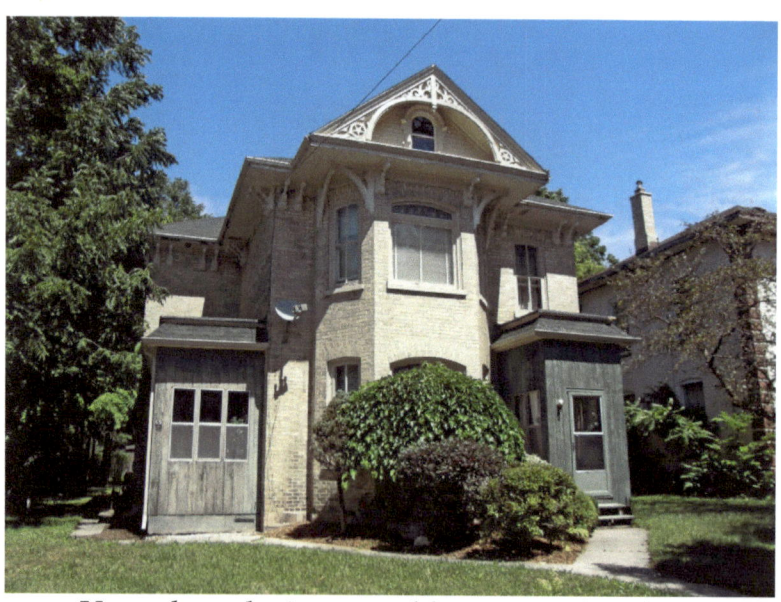

Verge board trim on gable, cornice brackets

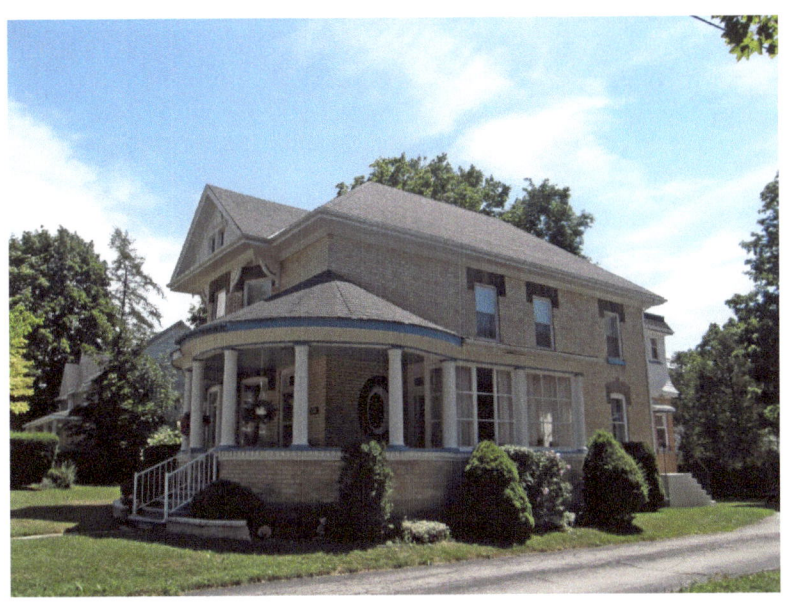

48 John Street – voussoirs and keystones, wraparound semicircular veranda

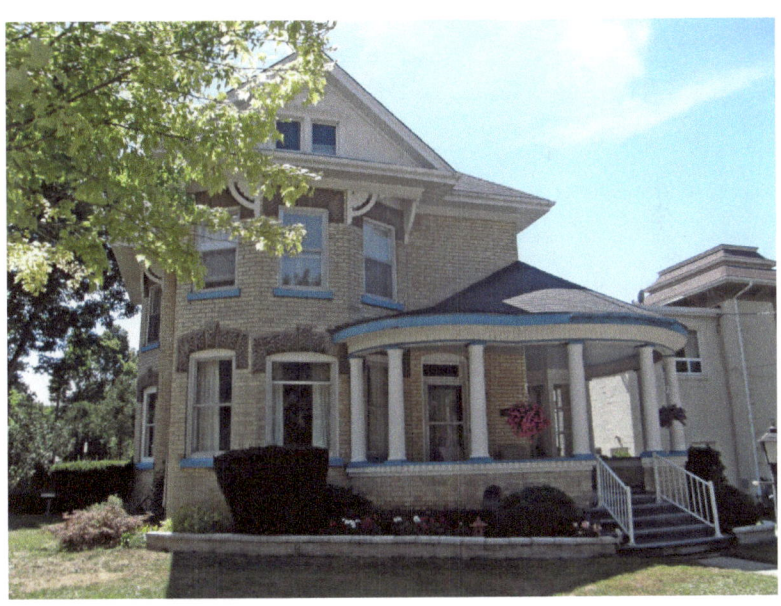

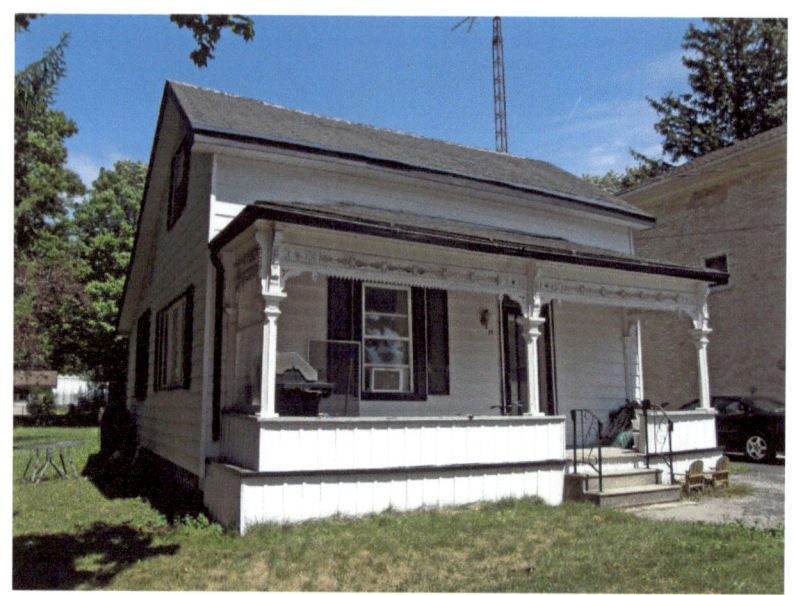
89 John Street – bric-a-brac on porch

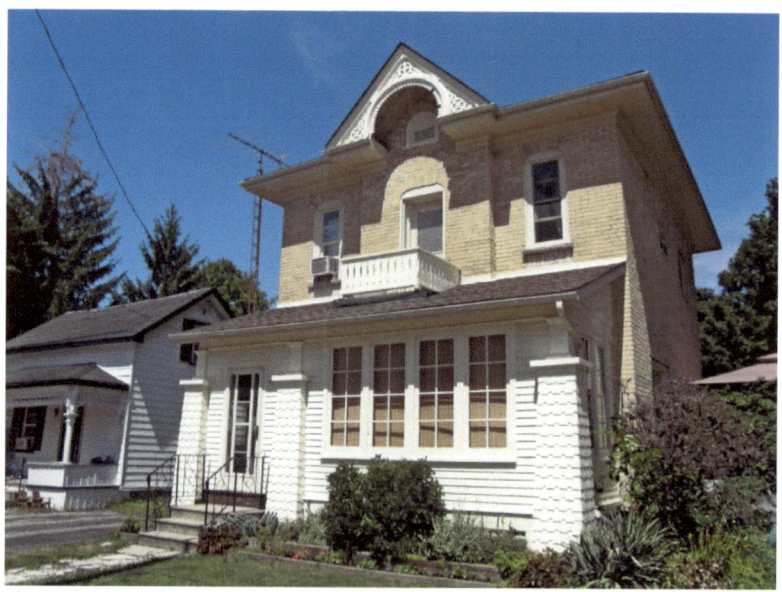
93 John Street – verge board trim on gable, second floor balcony

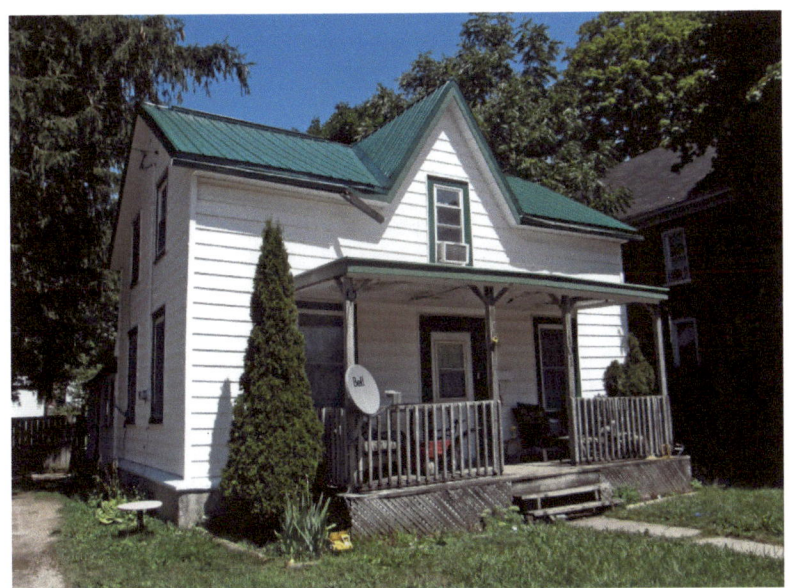

101 John Street - Gothic

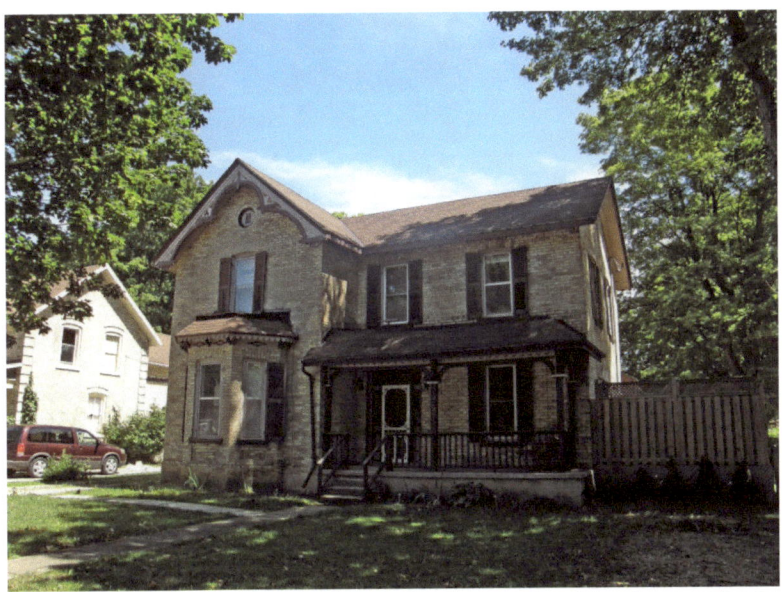

257 Shuter Street - verge board trim on gable, bay window

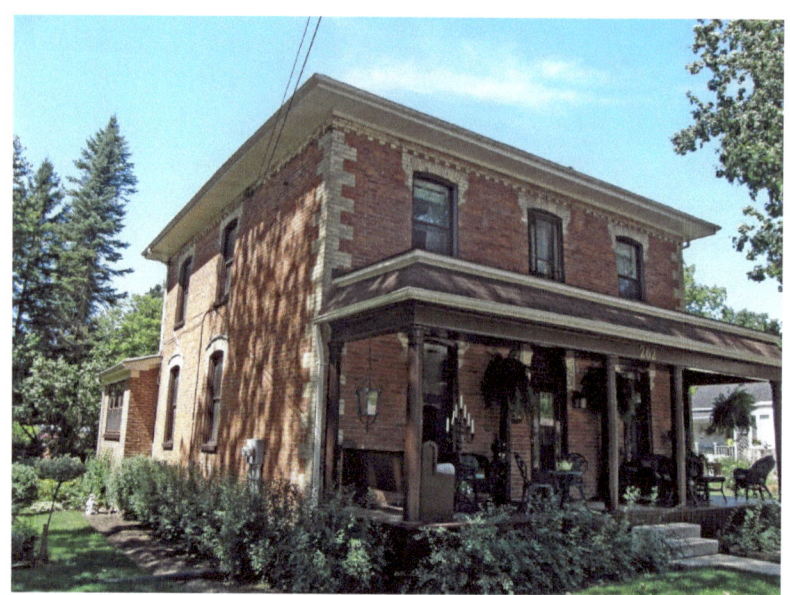

262 Shuter Street – contrasting corner quoins and voussoirs

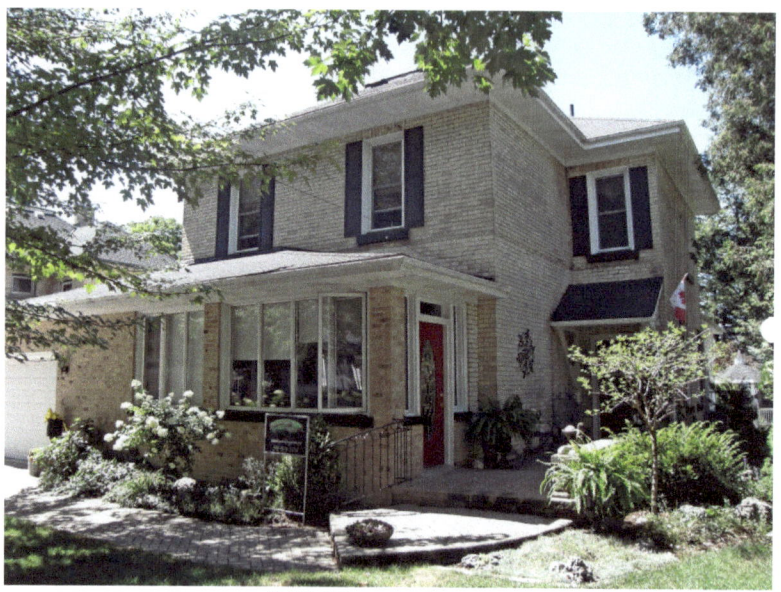

210 Shuter Street

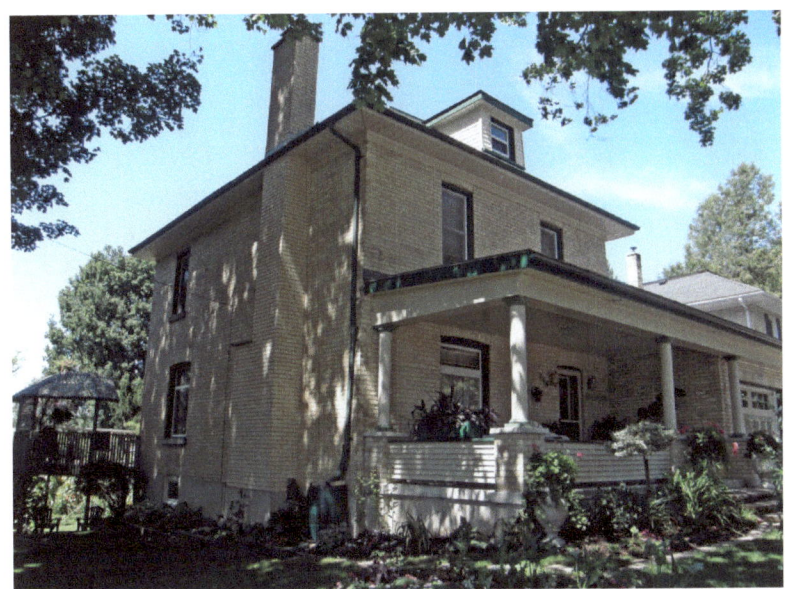

204 Shuter Street - dormer

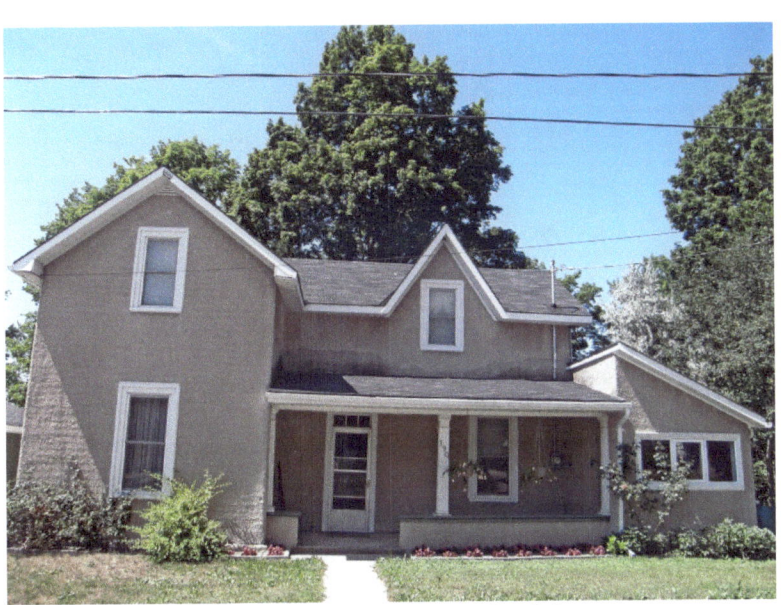

190 Shuter Street – Gothic

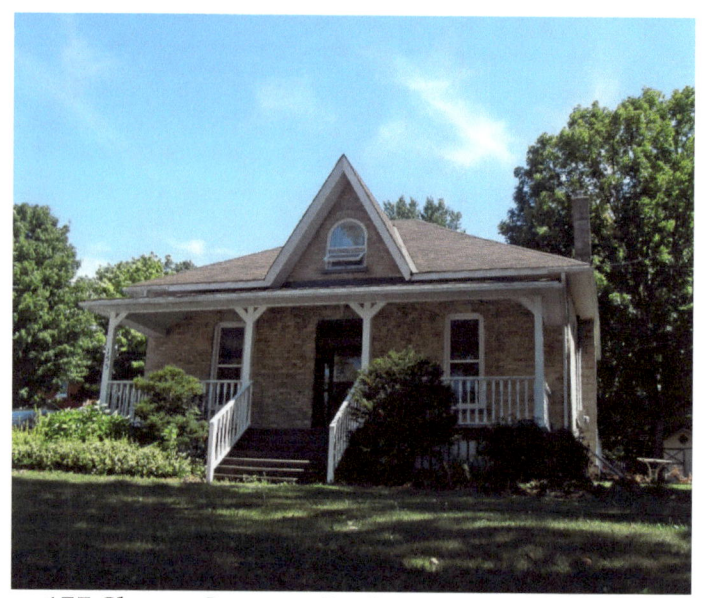

155 Shuter Street – Gothic Regency Cottage

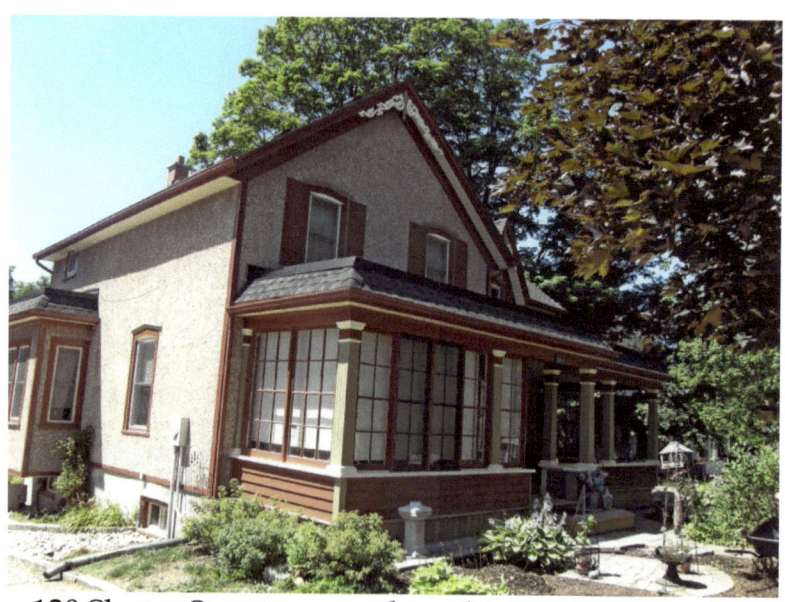

120 Shuter Street – verge board trim at top of gable

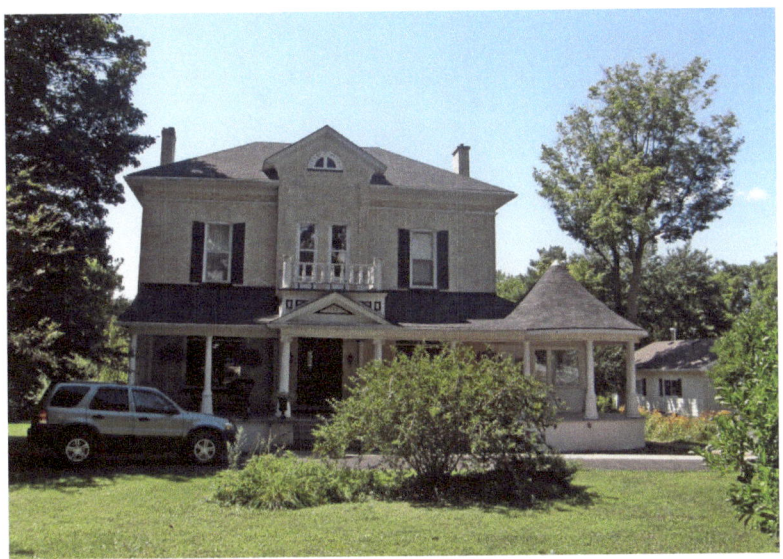

112 Shuter Street – hipped roof, 2½-story frontispiece, second floor balcony, Ionic porch pillars below pediment

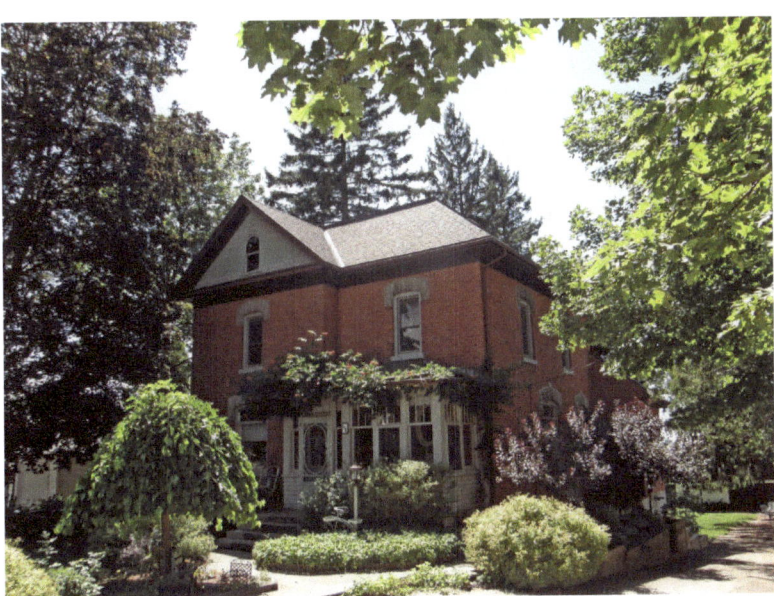

134 Shuter Street - voussoirs

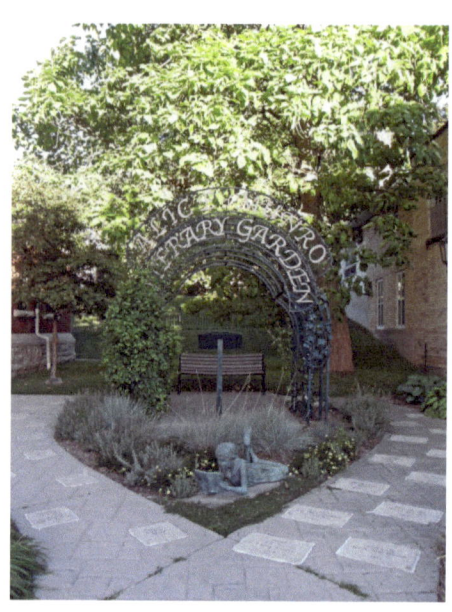

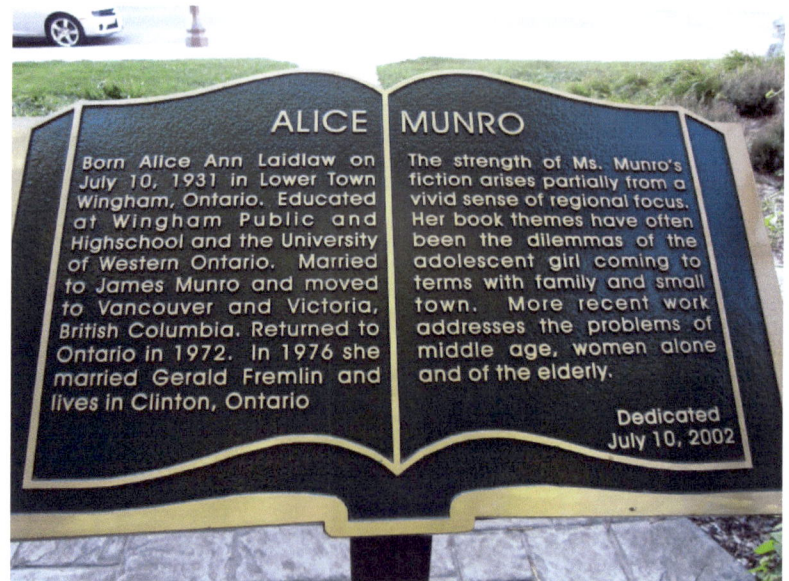

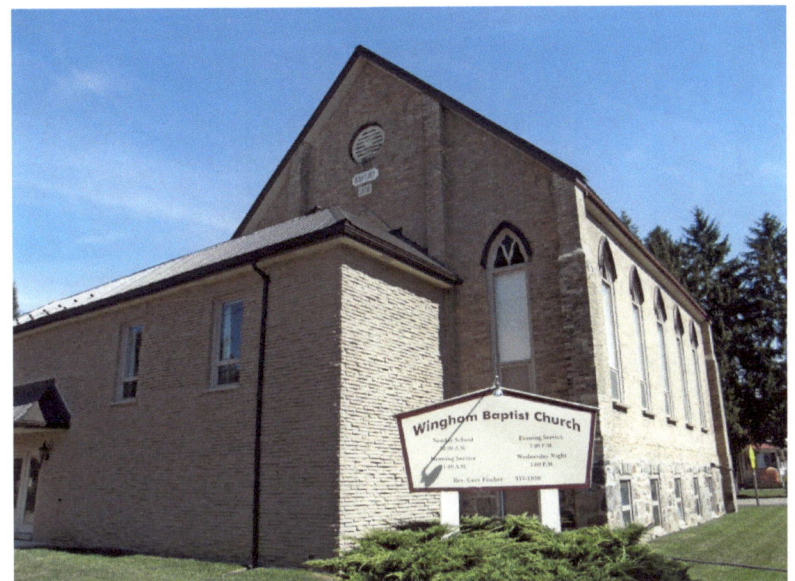

Wingham Baptist Church – 1876 – Gothic, lancet windows

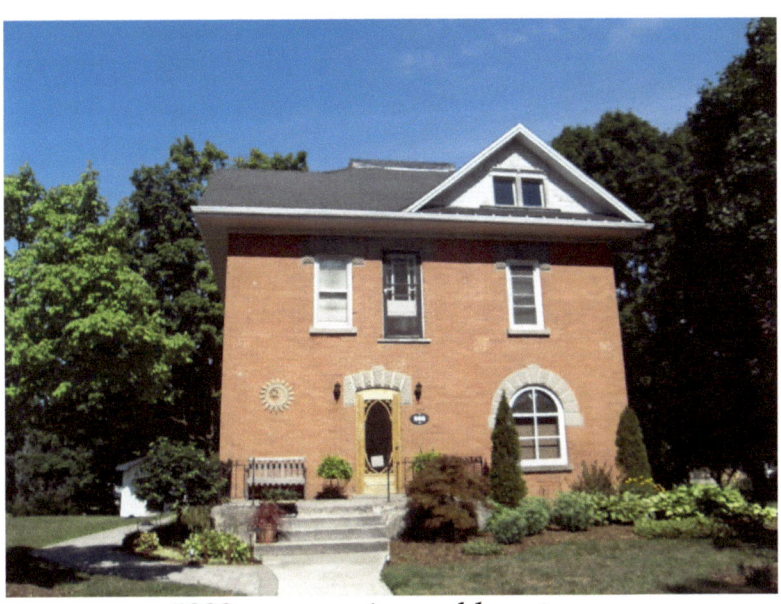

#232 – voussoirs and keystones

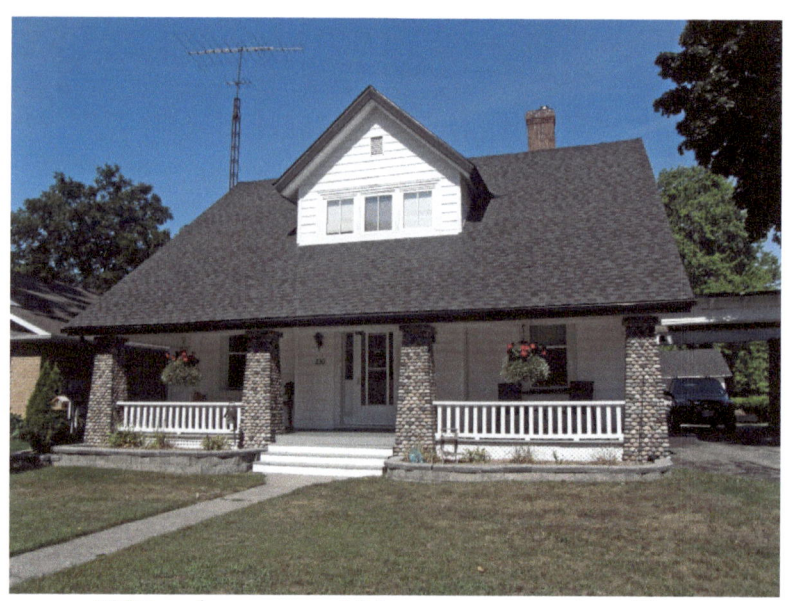
#230 – dormer, cobblestone veranda pillars

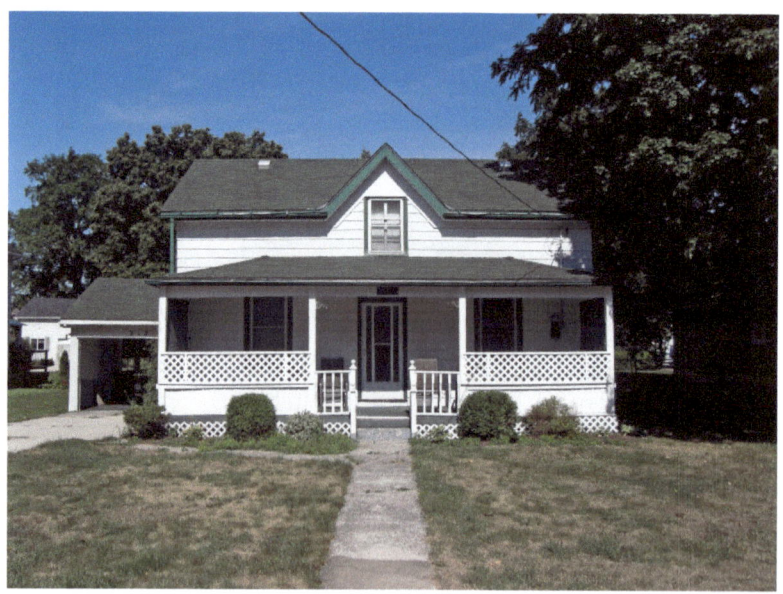
#218 – Gothic Regency Cottage

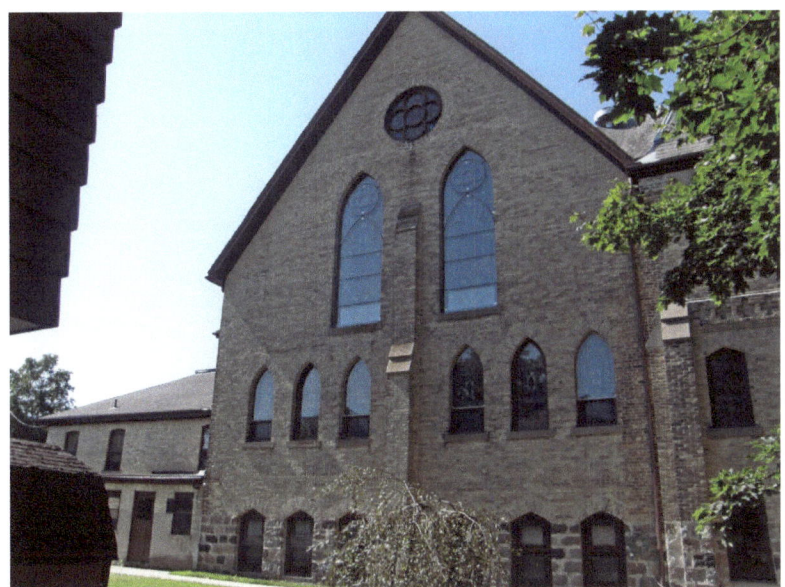
Rose window

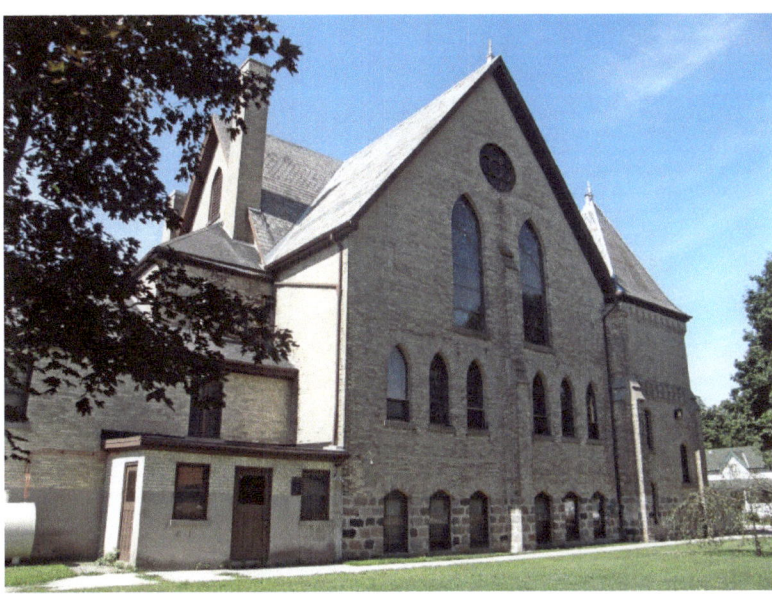
Dichromatic tile work on roof, buttresses, lancet windows

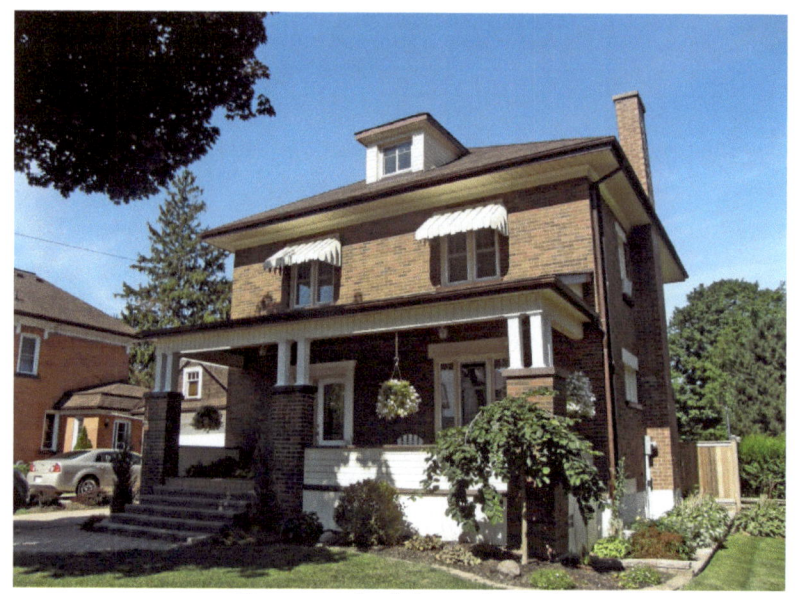

Dormer in hipped roof

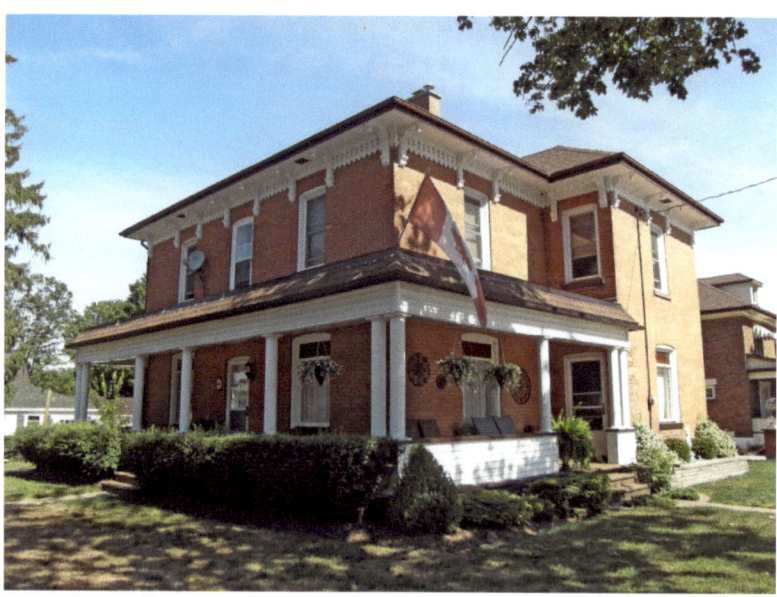

#69 – Italianate - hipped roof, cornice brackets

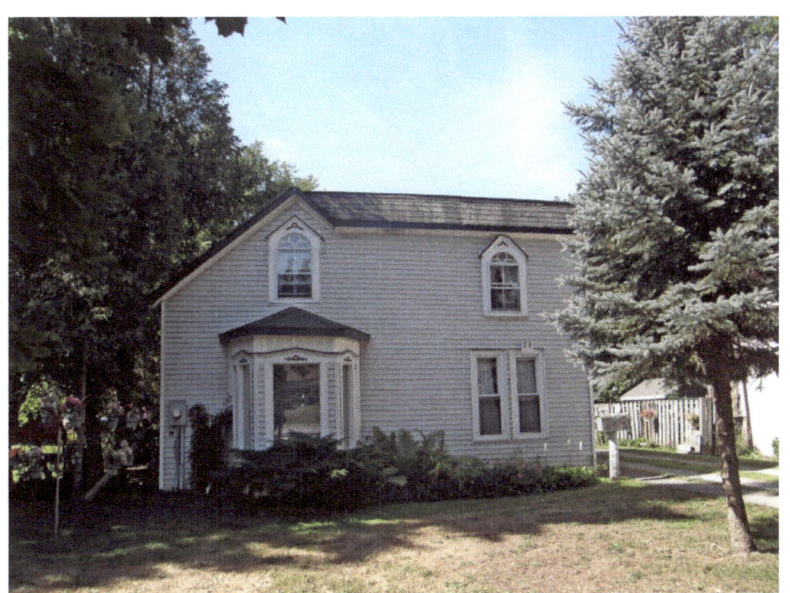

#74 - Vernacular – bay window

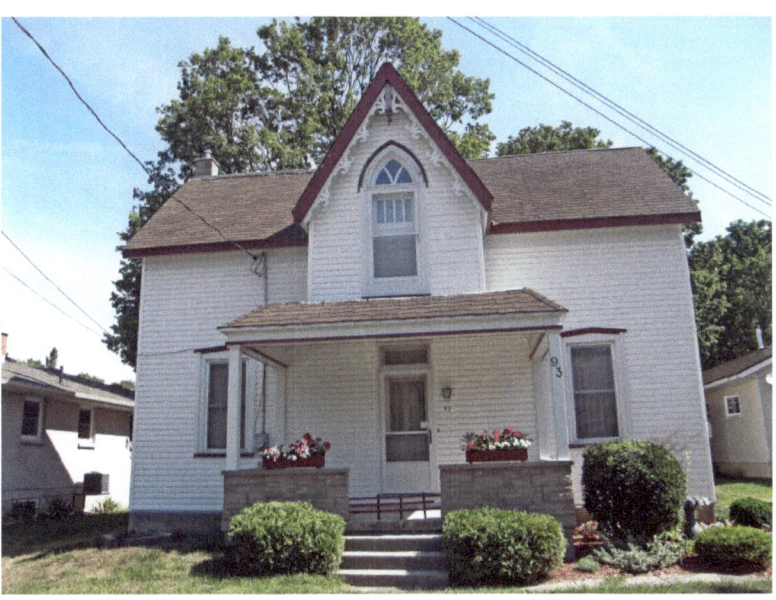

#93 - Gothic – verge board trim and finial on gable

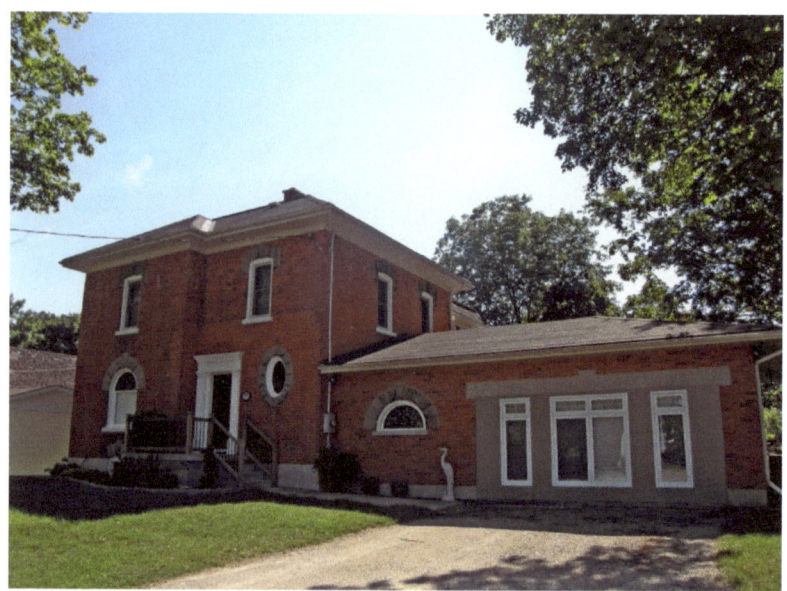

#199 – hipped roof, voussoirs and keystones, two-story main house with 1-story wing

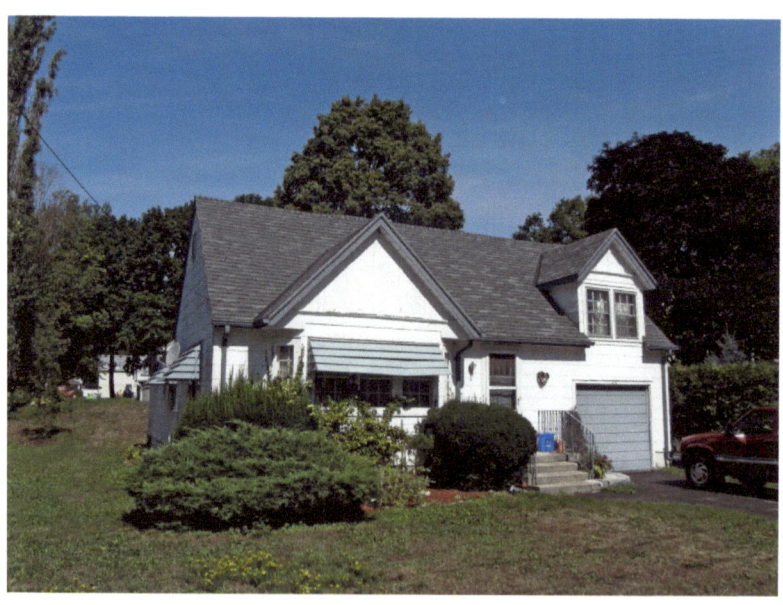

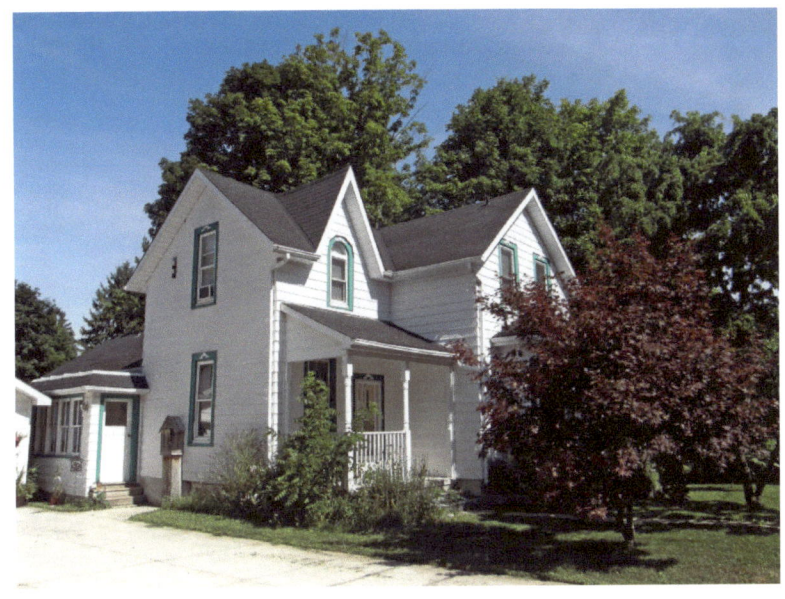

Gothic

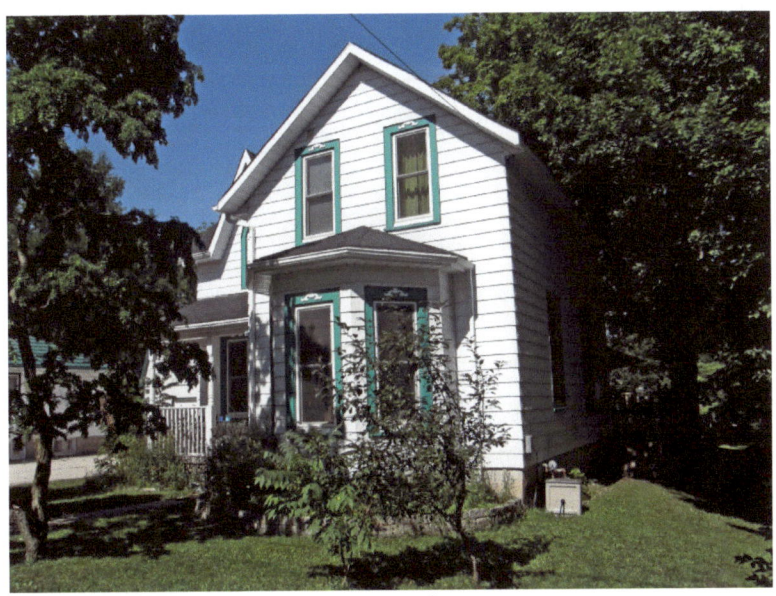

Bay window

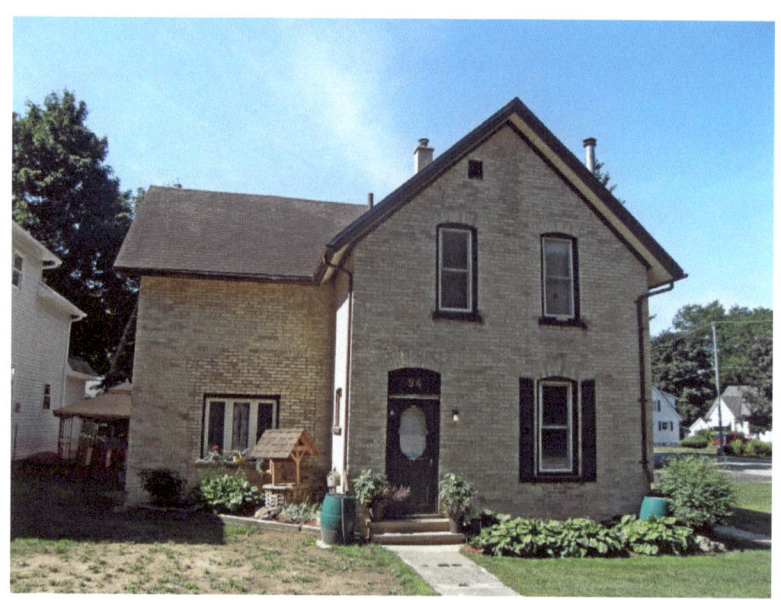

#94 - Gothic

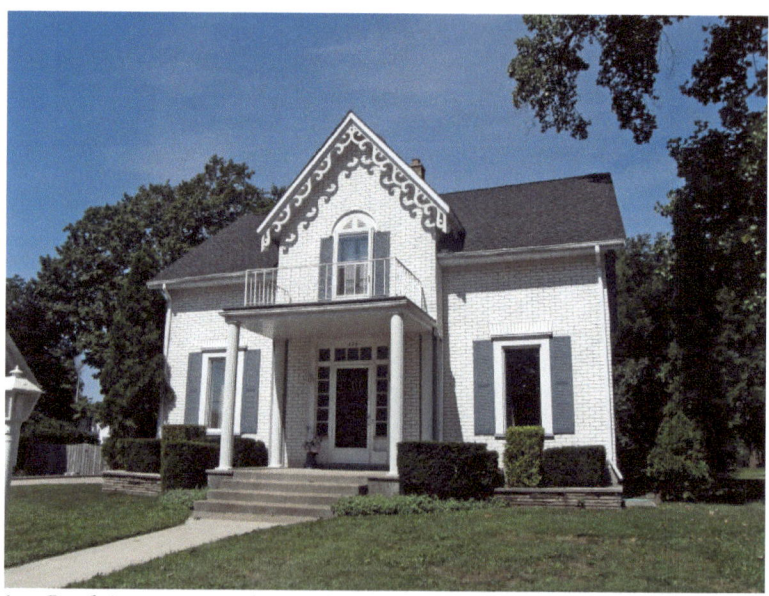

#326 - Gothic – verge board trim on gable, second floor balcony, sidelights and transom windows

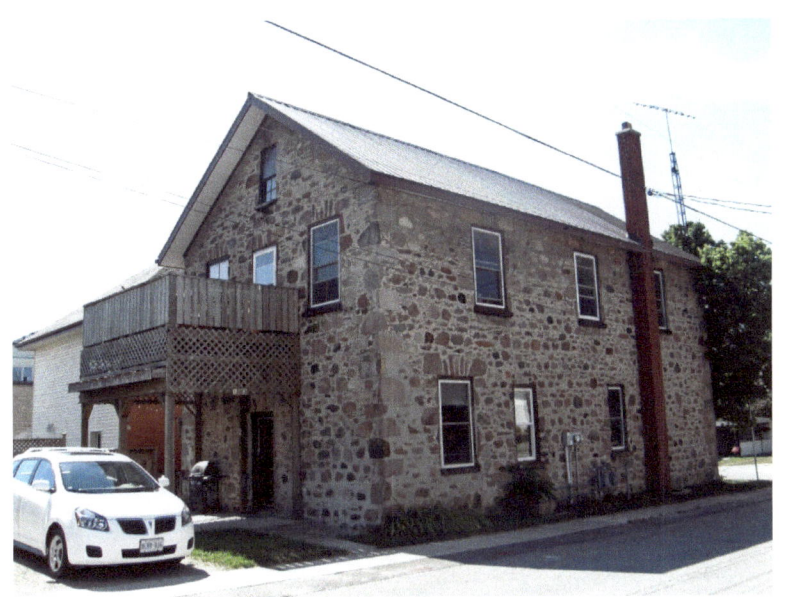

#183 – stone building

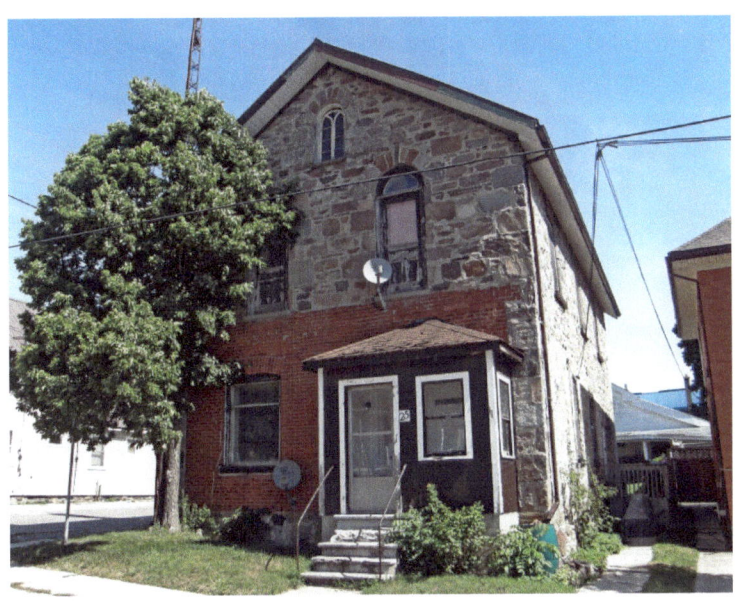

#25 - voussoirs

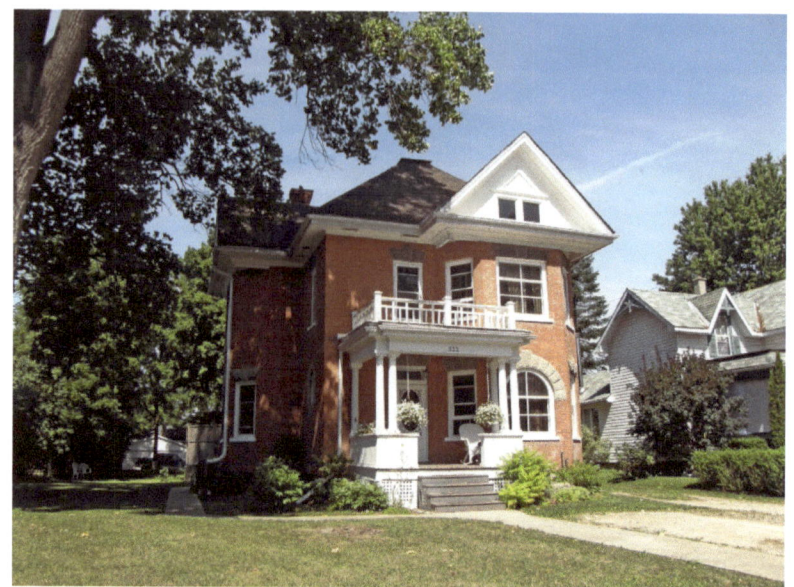

#332 – voussoirs and keystones, second floor balcony

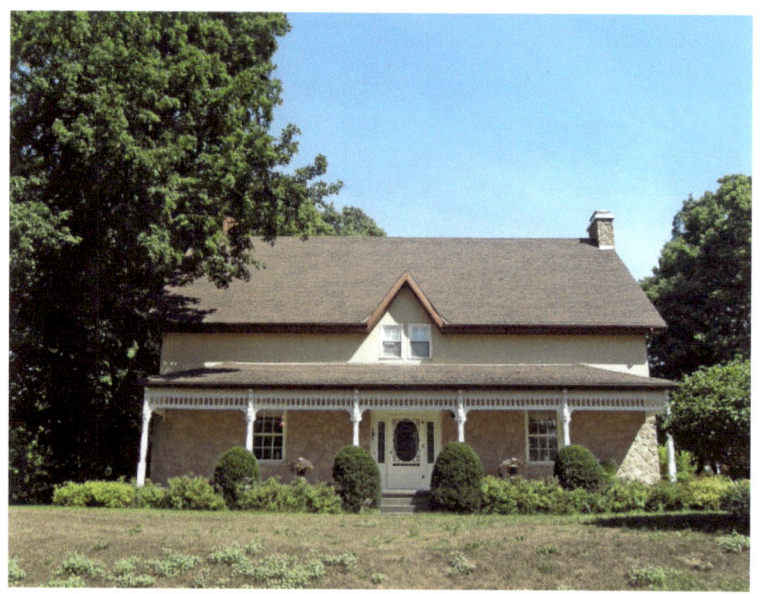

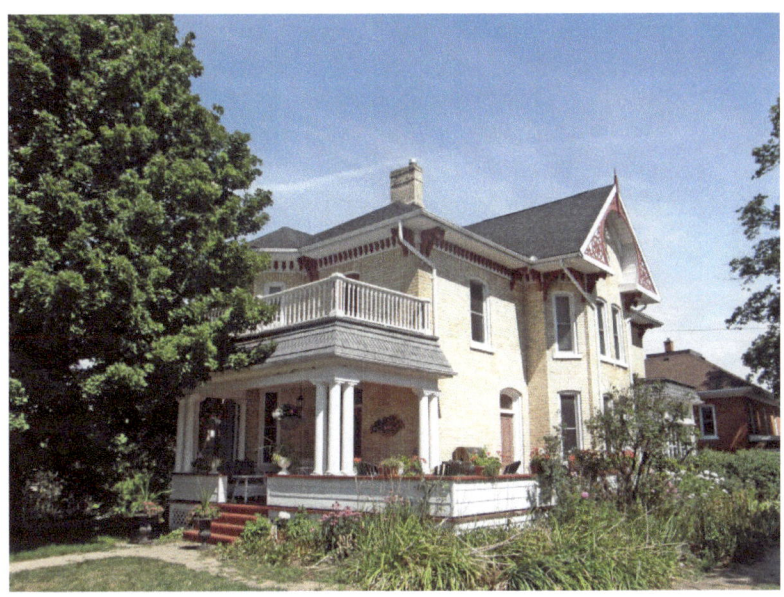

Cornice brackets, verge board trim and finial on gable, Doric pillars

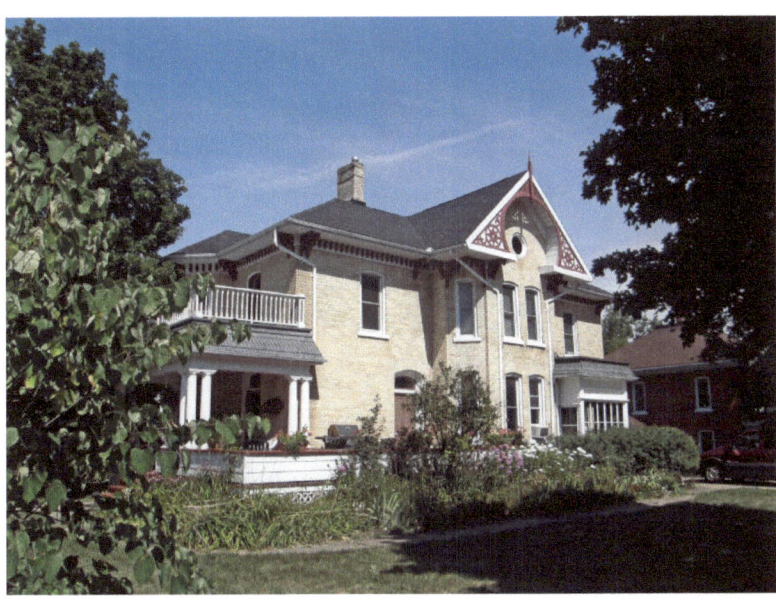

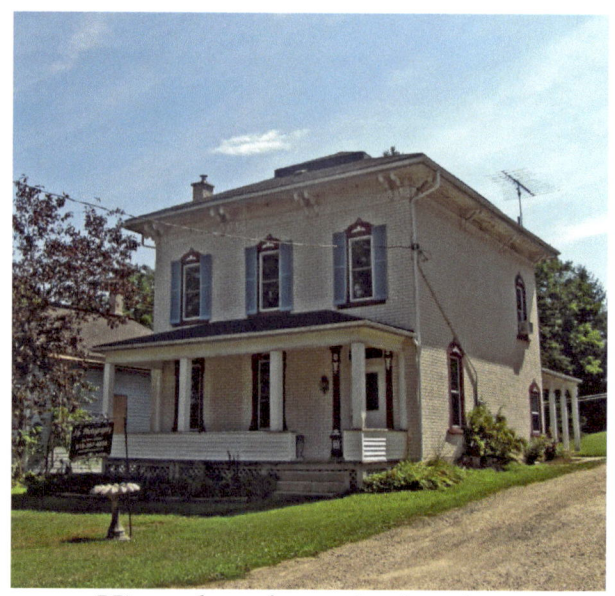
Hipped roof, cornice brackets

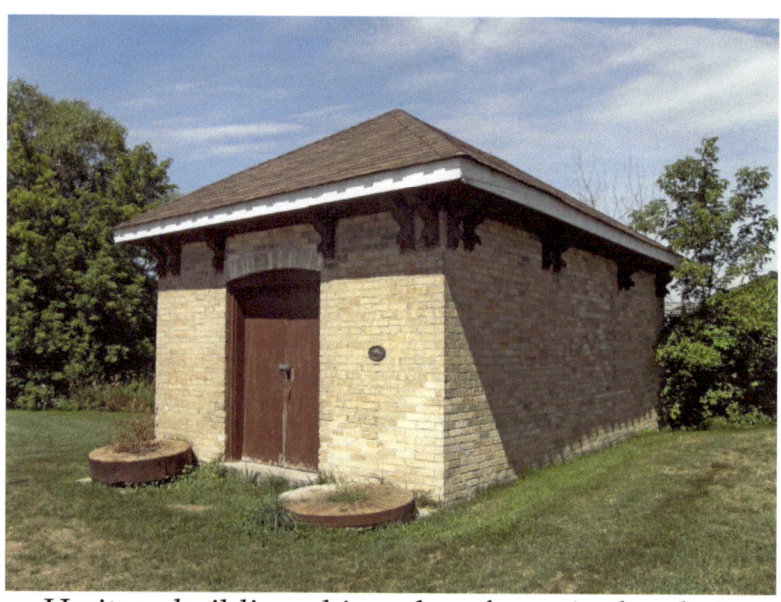
Heritage building - hipped roof, cornice brackets

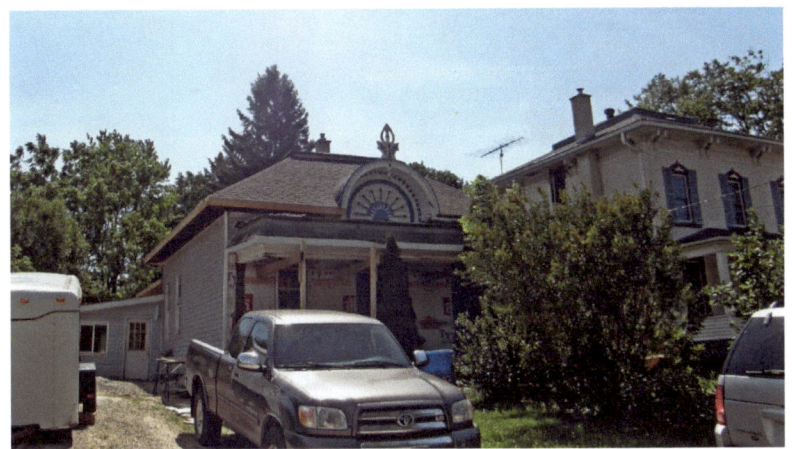

Hipped roof

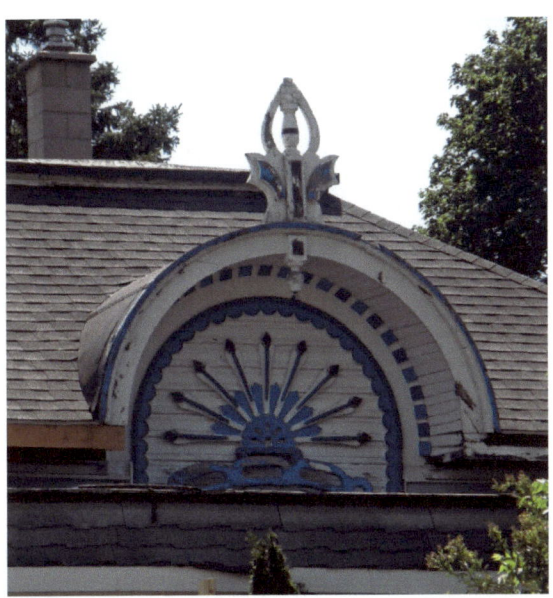

Semicircular pediment with decorated tympanum topped with a finial

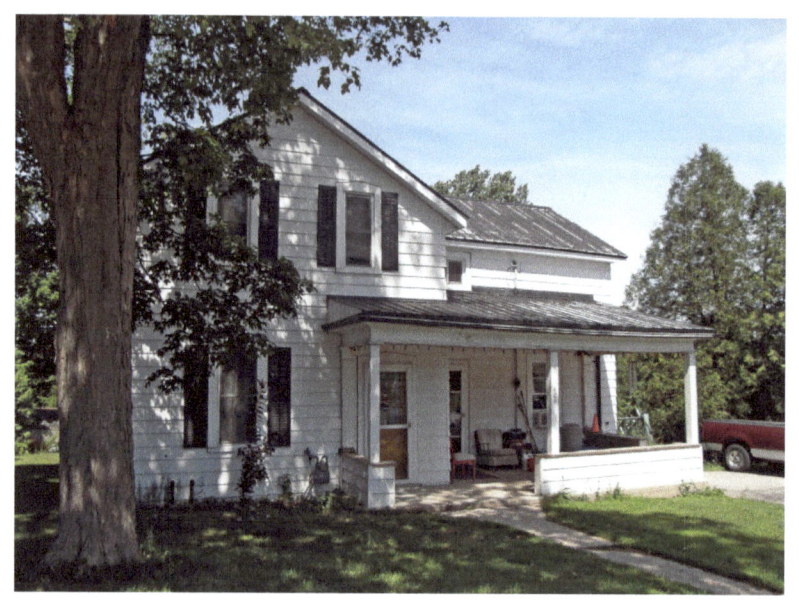

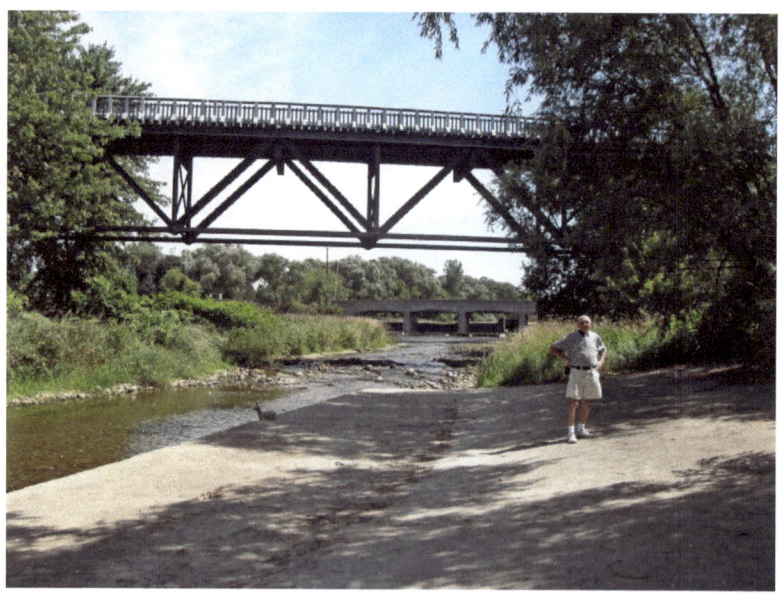

Auburn

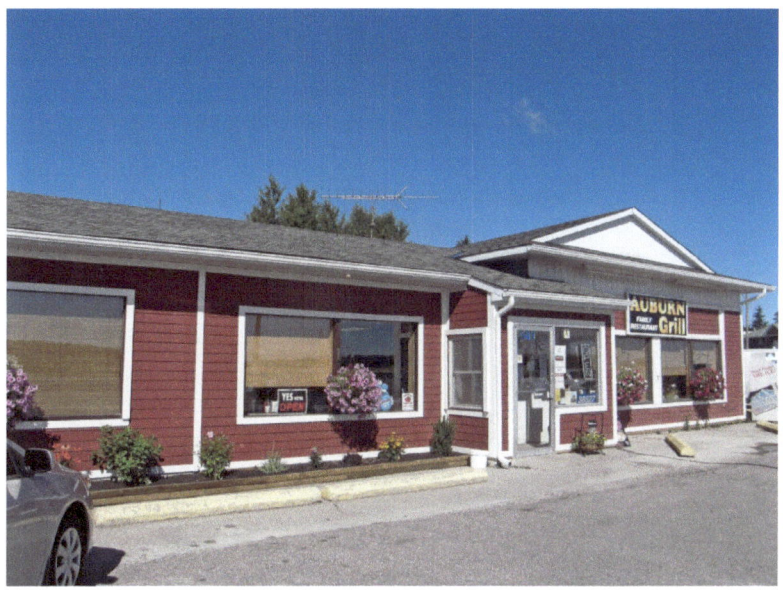

Auburn Grill Family Restaurant

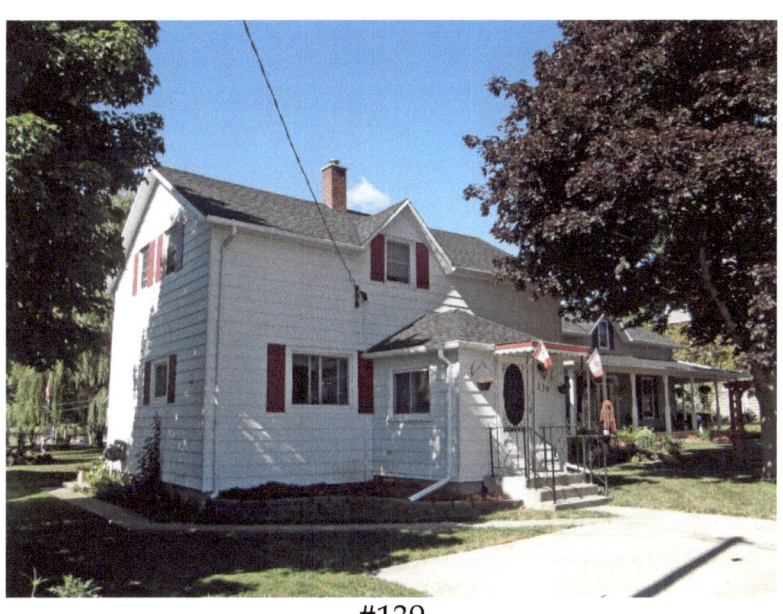

#139

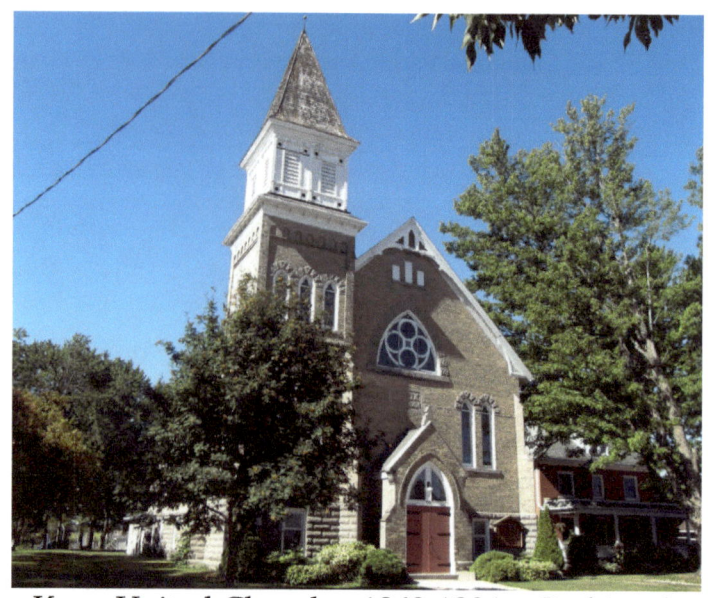

Auburn Knox United Church – 1860-1904 – Gothic – lancet windows, voussoirs, rose window, 3½-story tower

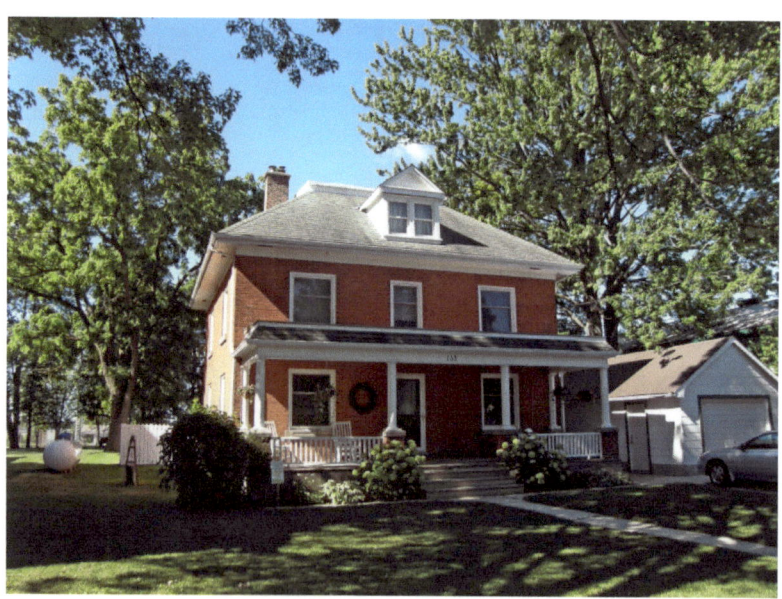

#133 – hipped roof with dormer

Belgrave

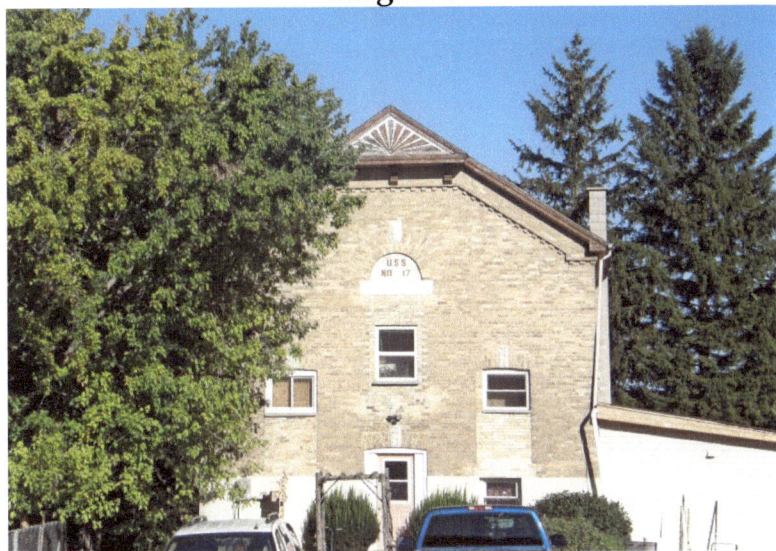

U. School Section No. 17 – voussoirs and keystone, trim on gable, cornice brackets, dentil molding

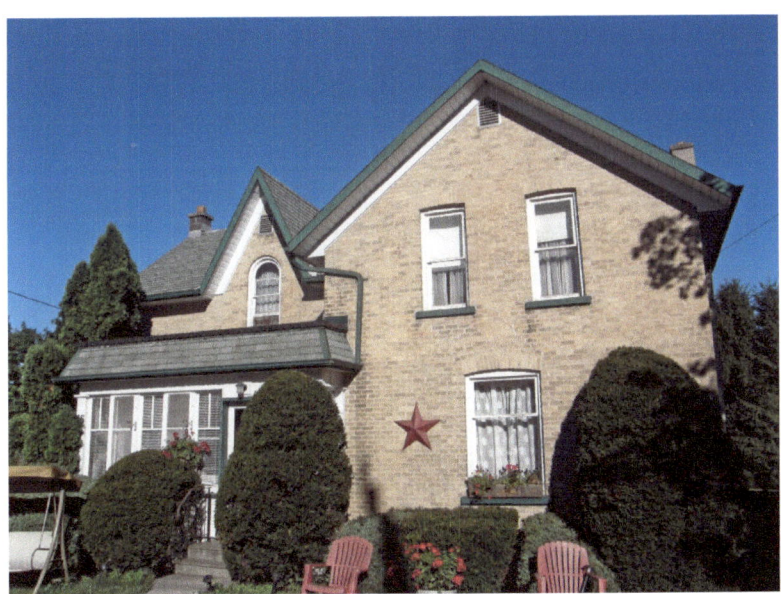

#16 - Gothic

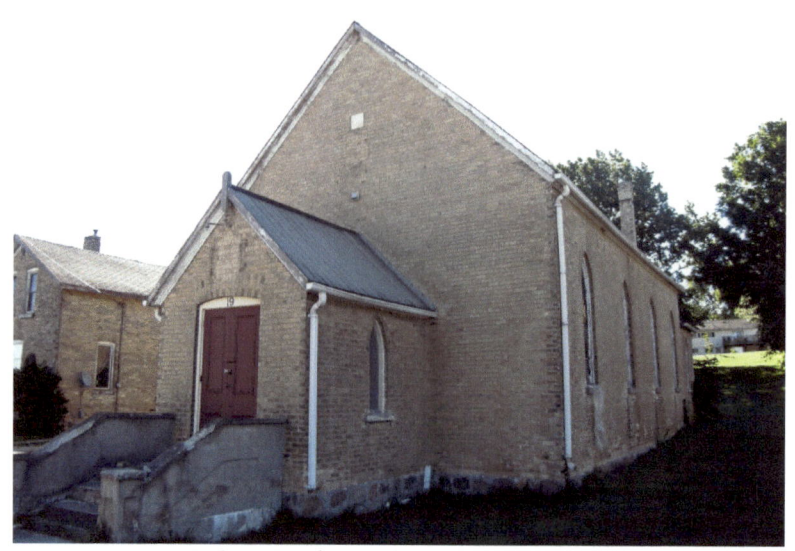

#19 – Gothic – lancet windows

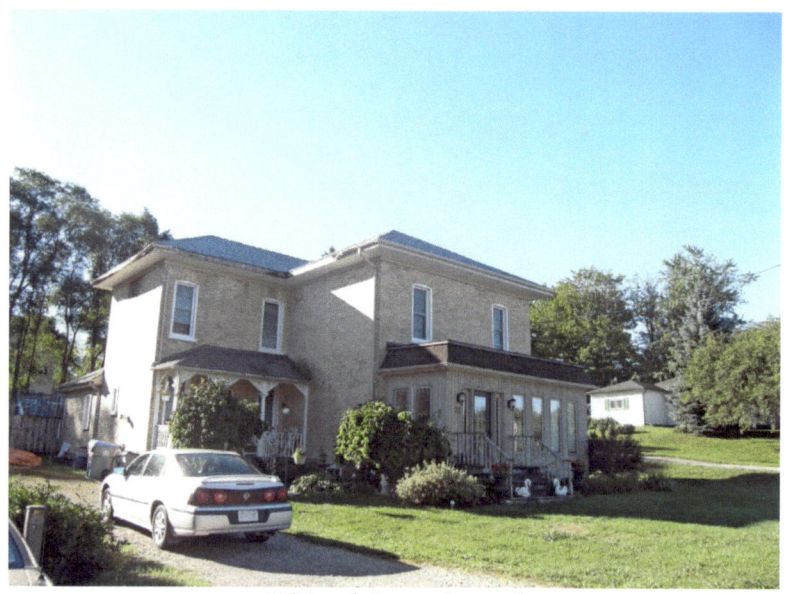

#21 – hipped roof

Blyth

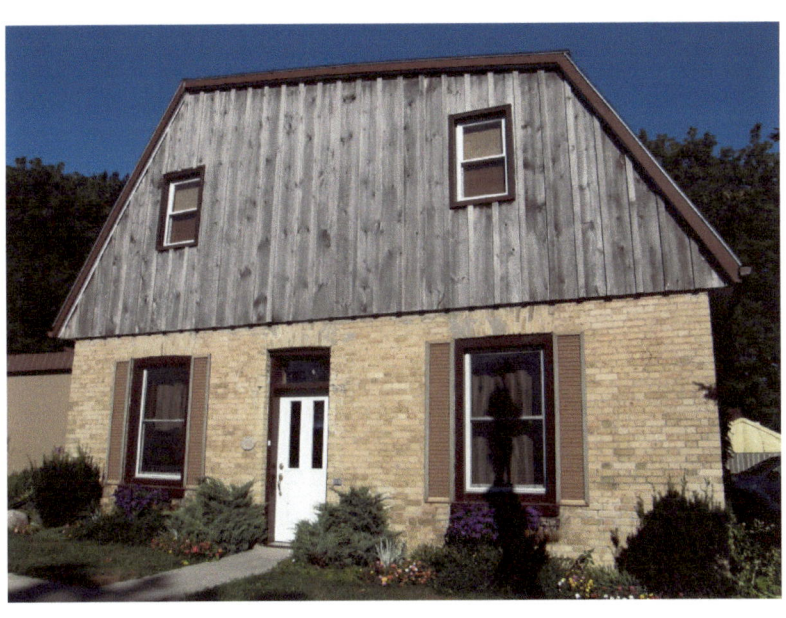

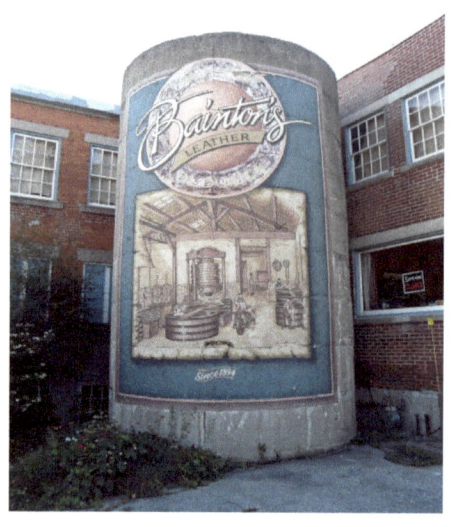

Bainton's Leather – since 1894

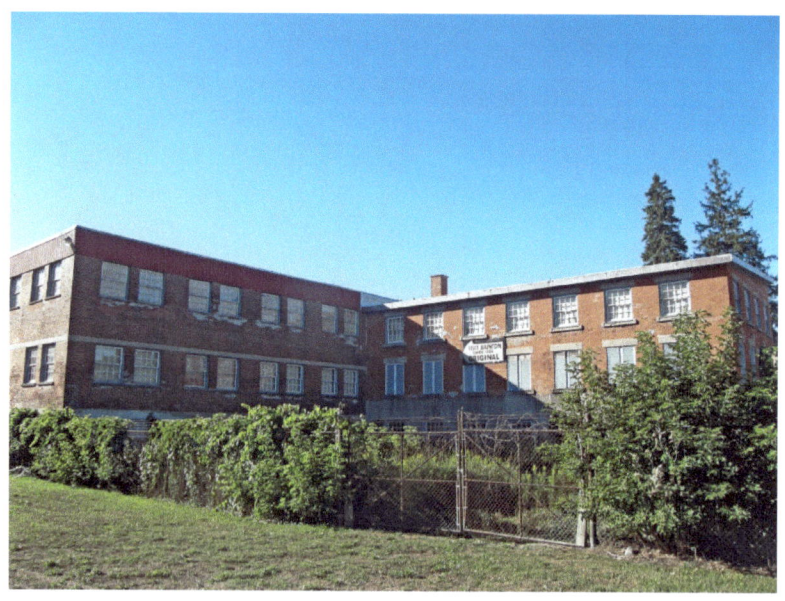

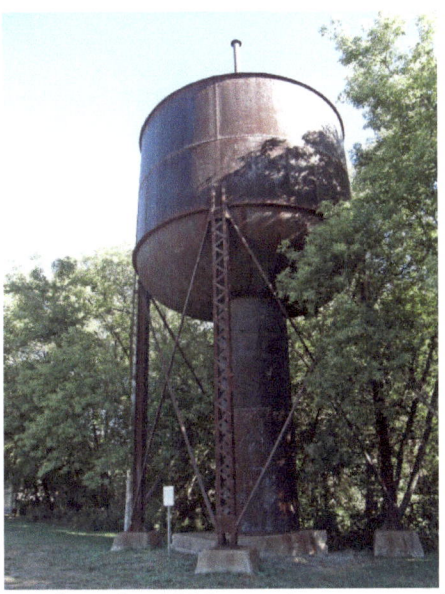

In the late 1800s and early 1900s, trains stopped at water towers like this to fill their reservoirs. The power generated by the steam drove the engines.

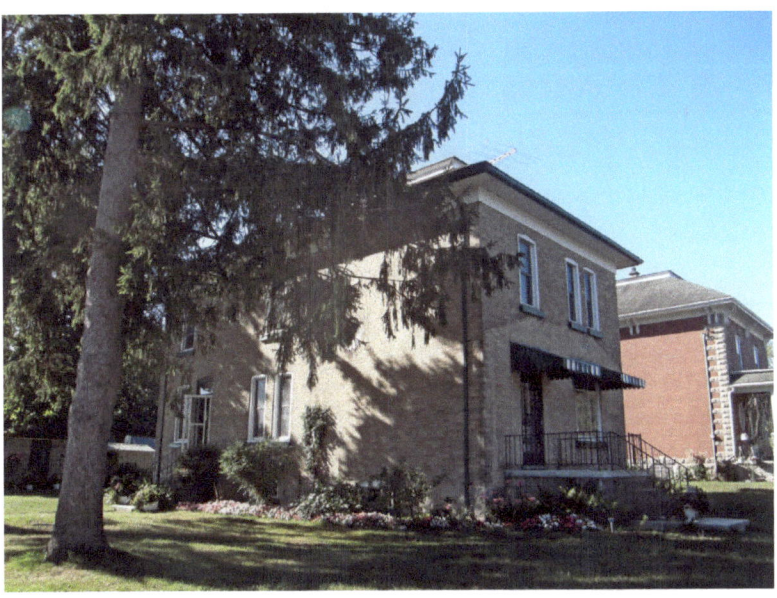

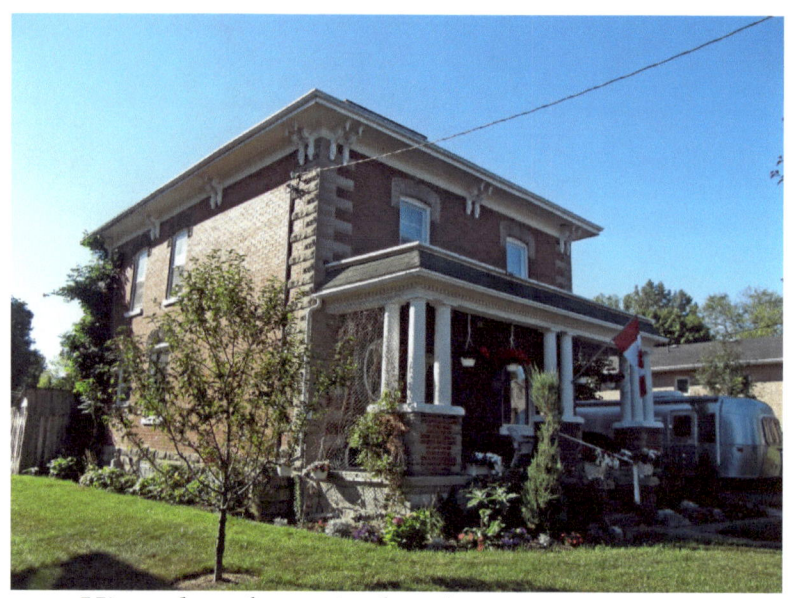

Hipped roof, cornice brackets, corner quoins

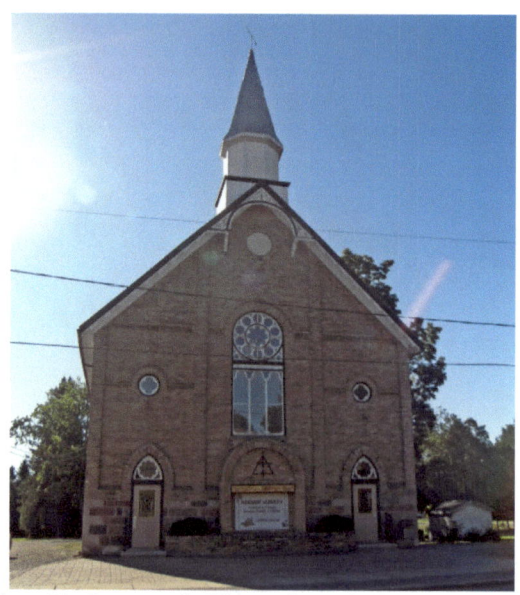

Blyth Christian Reformed Church – A.D. 1889 - pilasters, rose windows, cupola

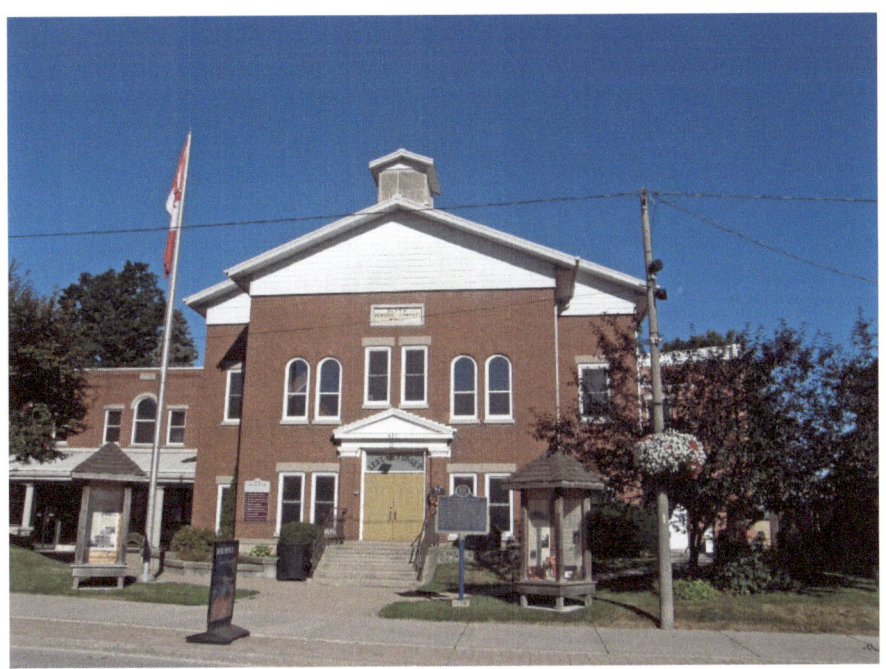

#431 – Blyth Memorial Community Hall - 1921

In 1975 Blyth Festival began when Blyth native James Roy returned to create a theatre that would deal with stories that speak to the rural and small-town people of the region. He began with a production created from the books of Harry J. Boyle who grew up near Auburn. "Mostly in Clover" set the Festival on its path of creating new plays since there were no plays created for rural Ontarians. Over the years, Memorial Hall has become the entertainment center of Huron County.

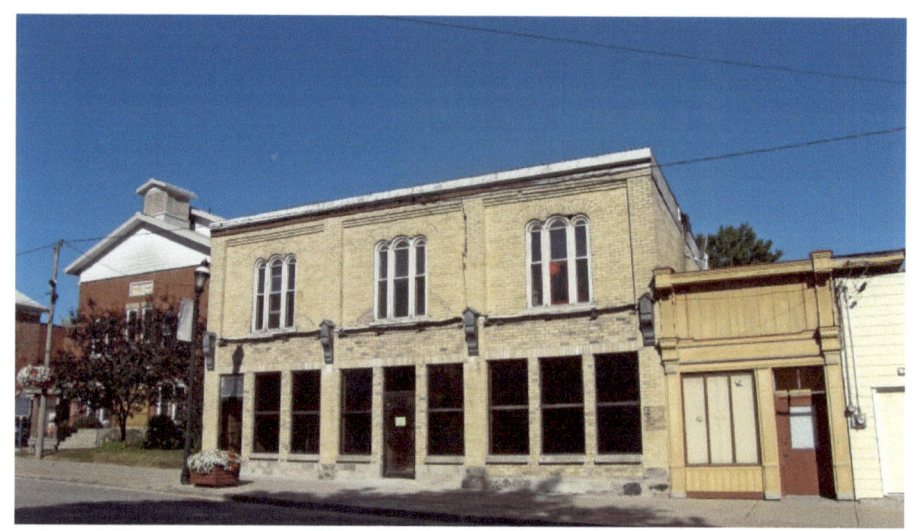

Voussoirs, pilasters

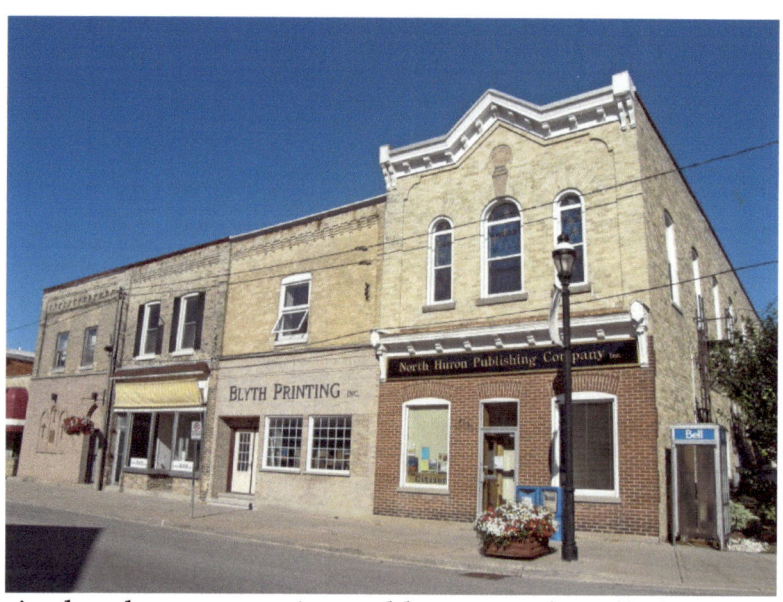

Cornice brackets, voussoirs and keystone, bevelled dentil molding

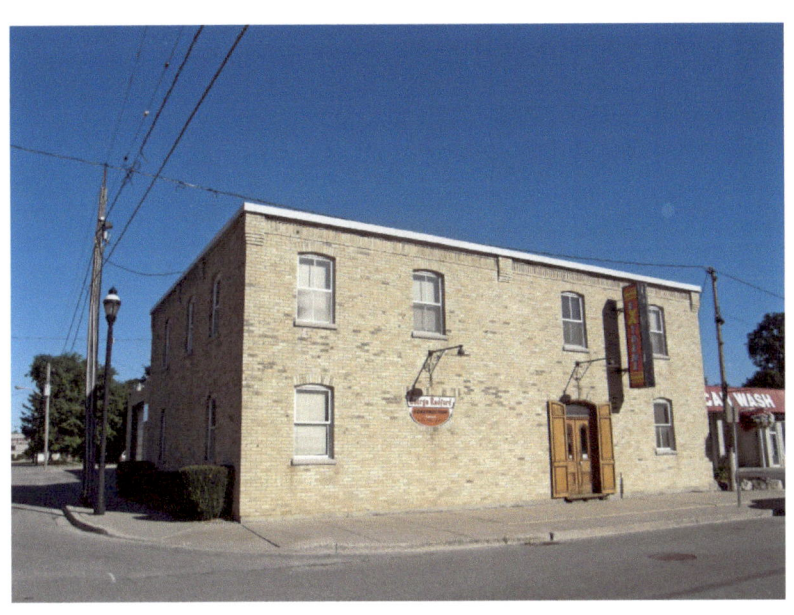

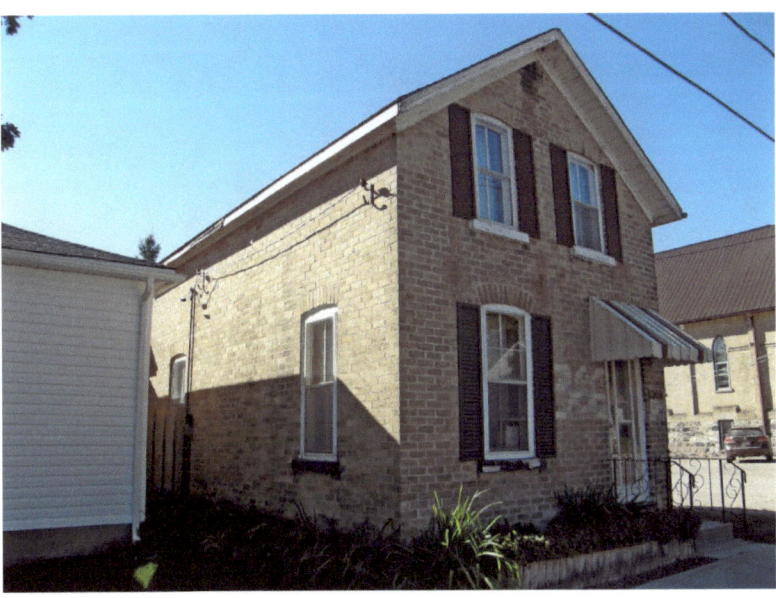

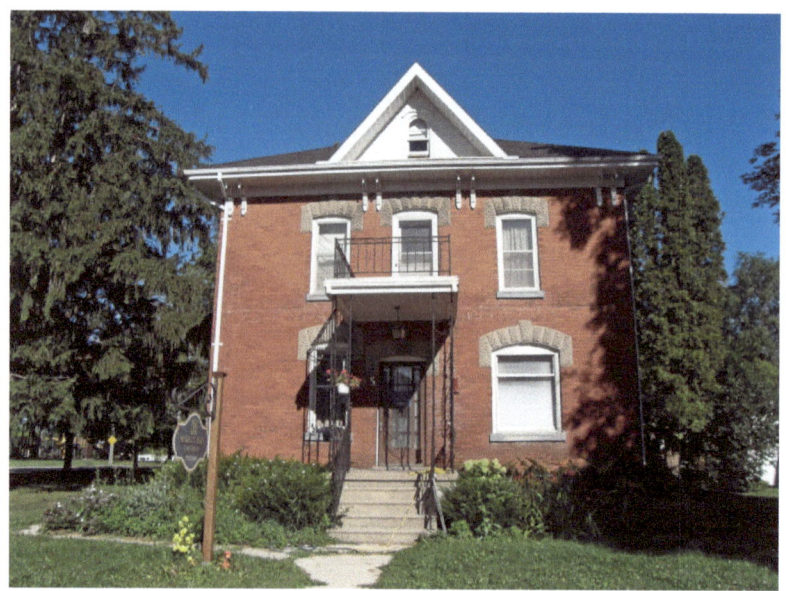

Cornice brackets, second floor balcony, voussoirs and keystones

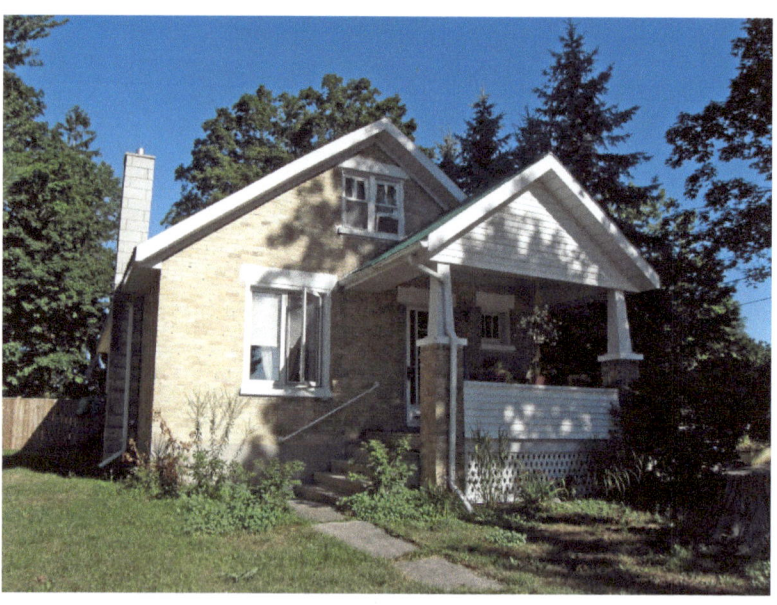

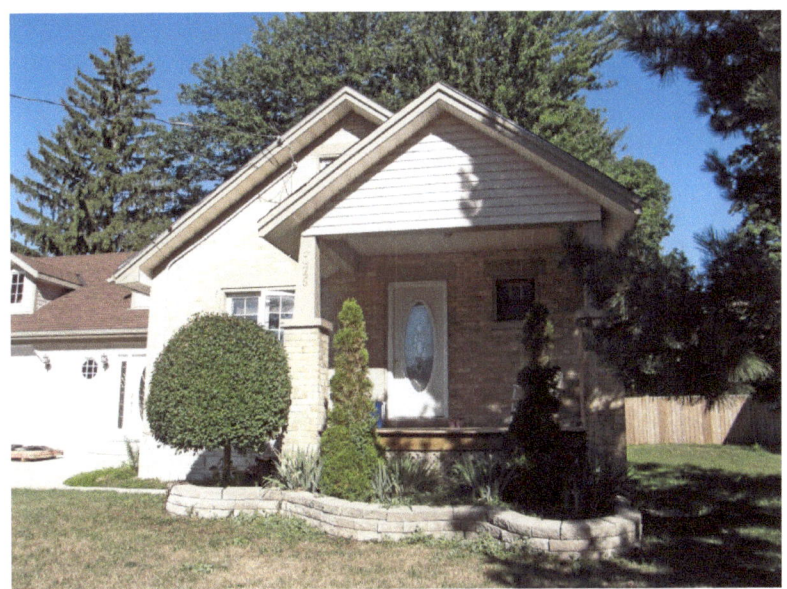

#325

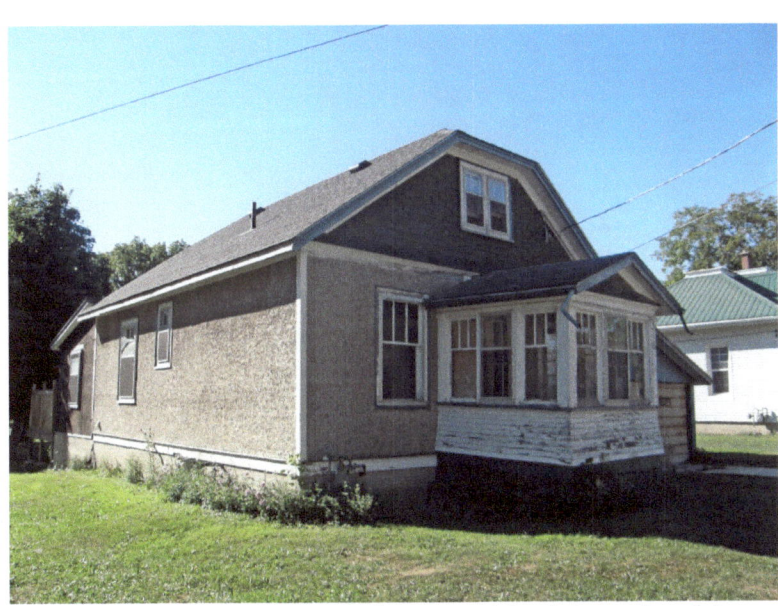

#318 - 1½-story stucco home with chipped gable

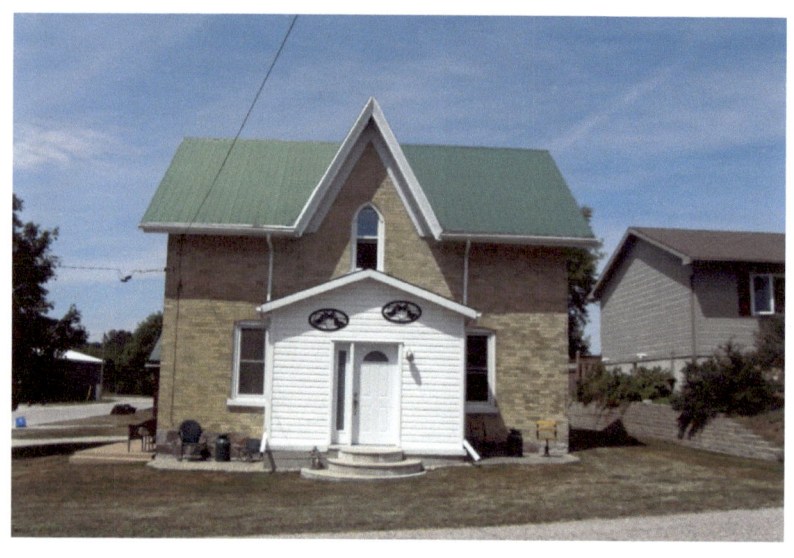

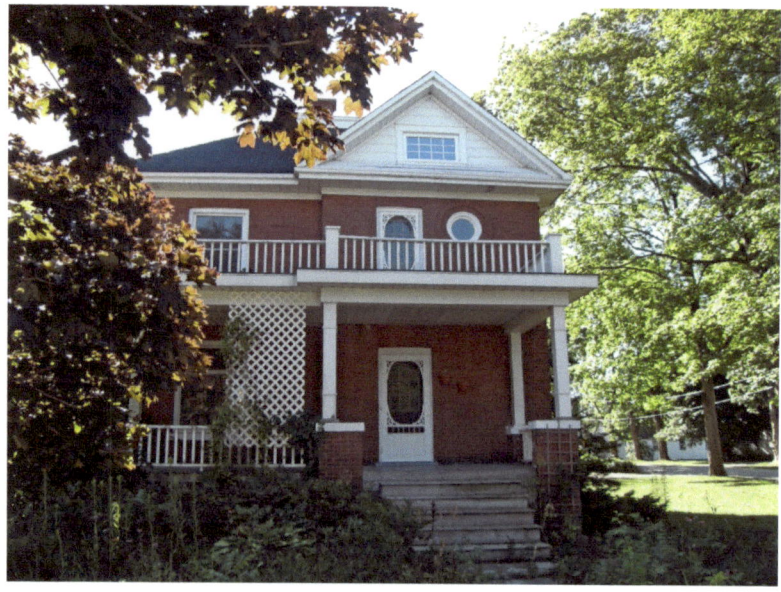

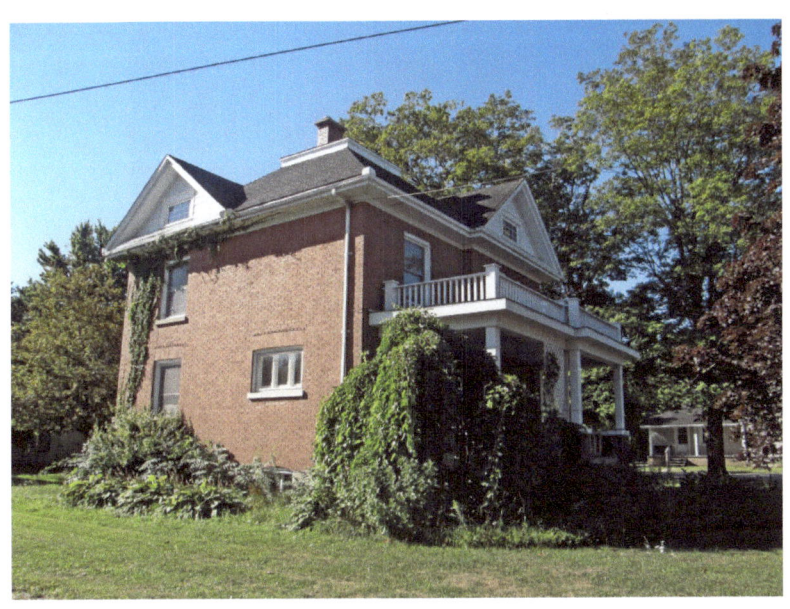

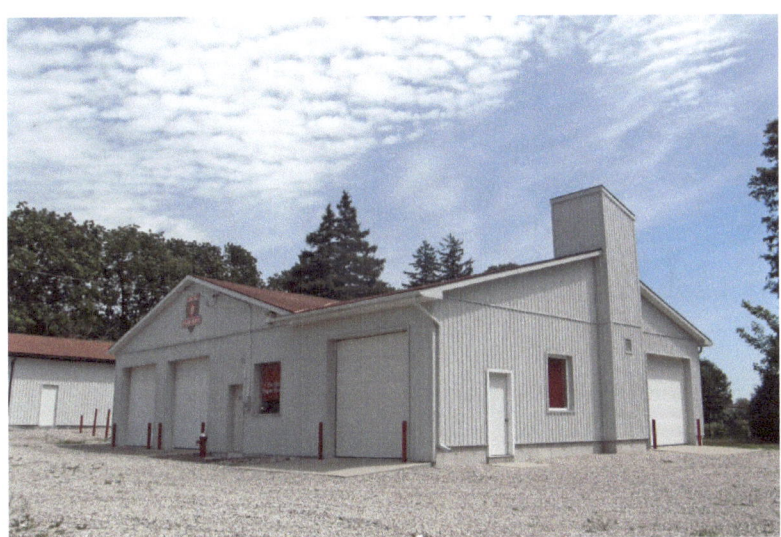

The Old Engine House

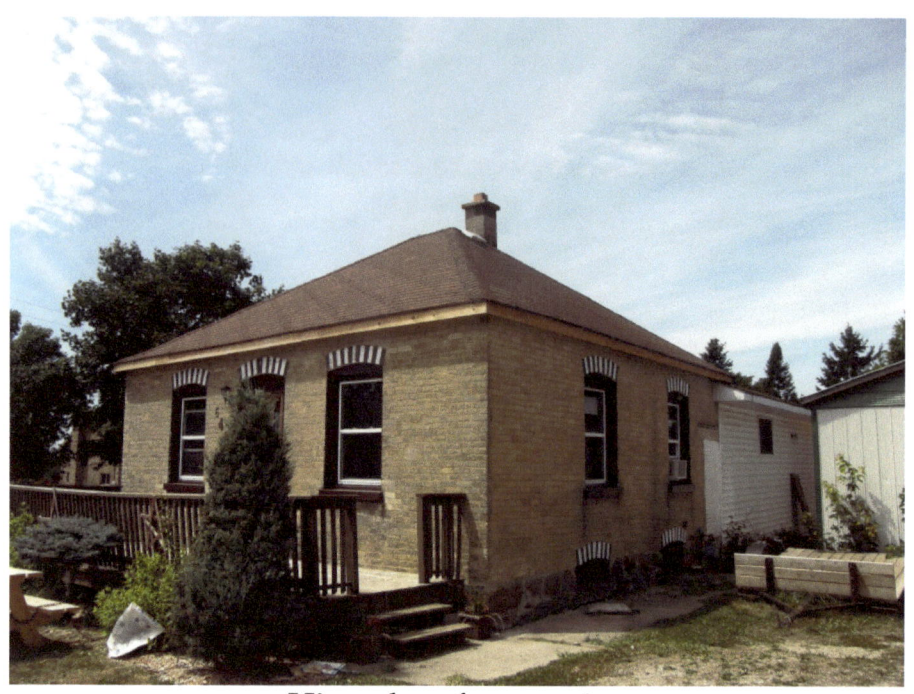
Hipped roof, voussoirs

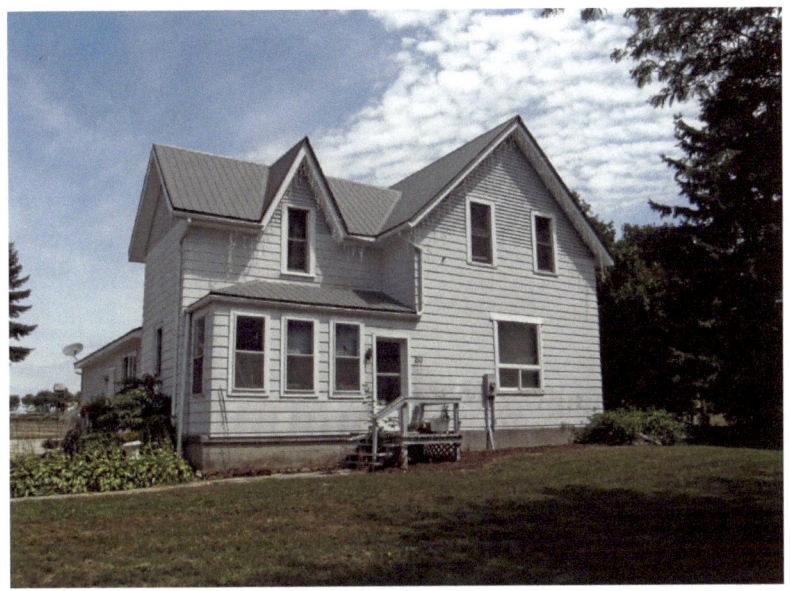

Gothic

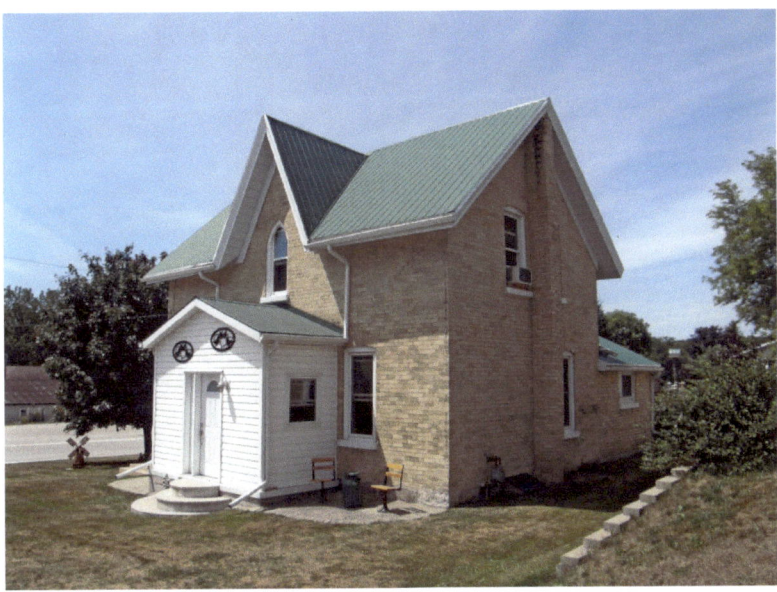

Gothic

Carlow

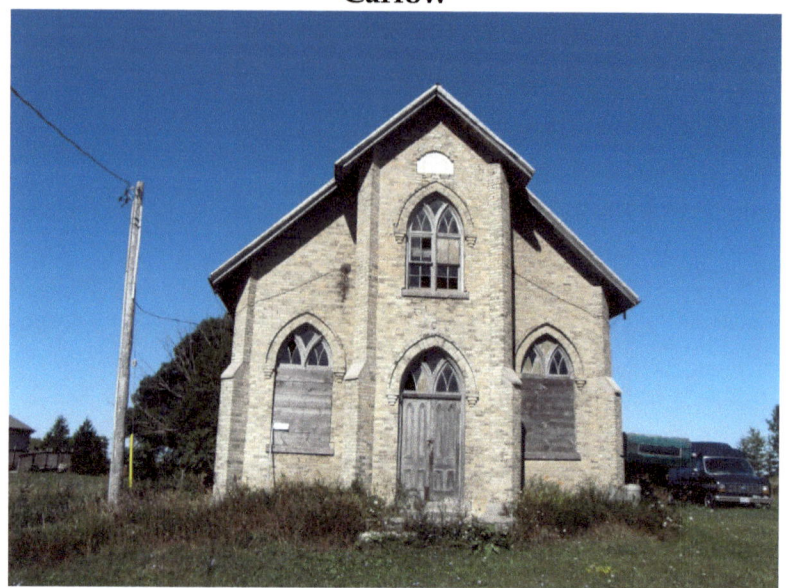

Carlow Presbyterian Church erected 1872

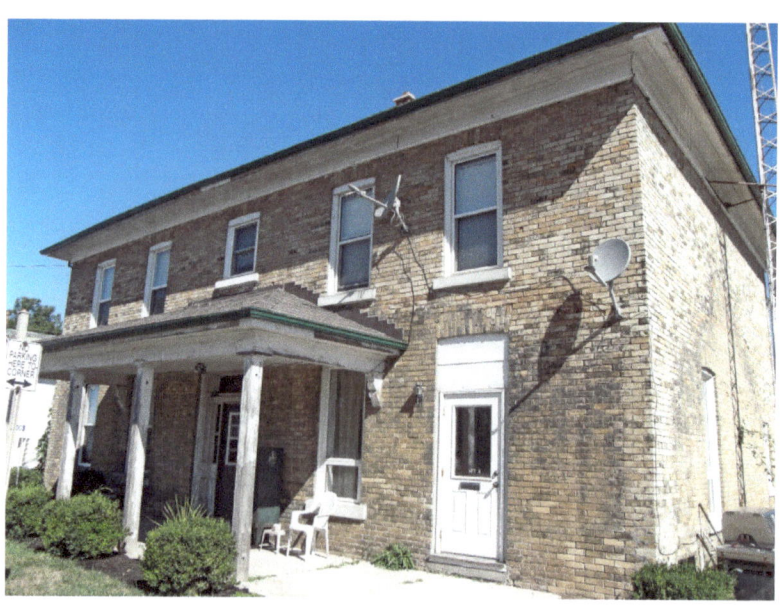

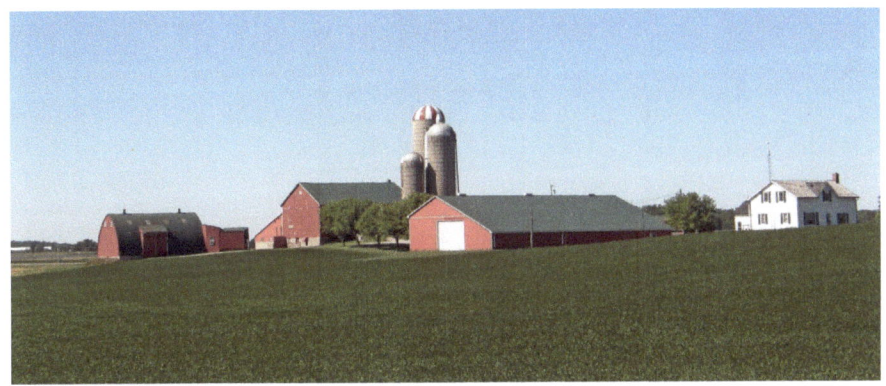

Farm

Dunlop

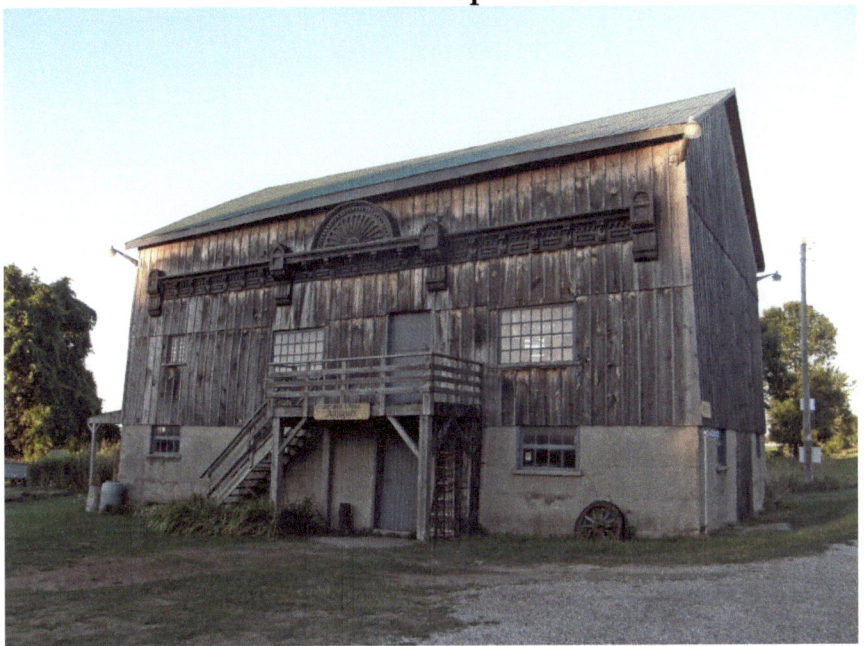

Antiques

Architectural Terms

Banding: Different materials, colors or textures used in horizontal bands along a wall. Example: Josephine Street, Page 12, Wingham	
Bay Window: A window that projects out from a wall, in a semicircular, rectangular, or polygonal design. Used frequently in Gothic and Victorian designs. Example: #271, Page 19, Wingham	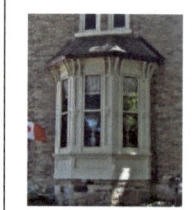
Brackets: a decorative or weight-bearing structural element which forms a right angle with one side against a wall and the other under a projecting surface such as an eave or roof. Example: 176 Josephine Street, Page 6, Wingham	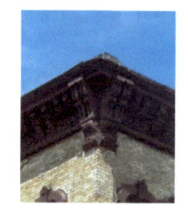
Buttress: a masonry structure built against or projecting from a wall which serves to support or reinforce the wall. In Canadian architecture, they are sometimes used for decoration. Example: 19 John Street East, Page 22, Wingham	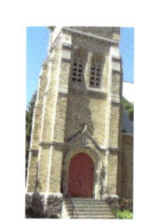
Cupola: A domed or curved roof rising from a building as a decorative element. Example: Blyth Christian Reformed Church, Page 53	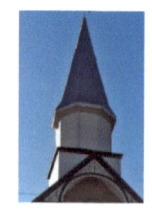

Dormer: (French for "sleep") a gable end window that pierces through the plane of a sloping roof surface to create usable space in the top floor or attic of a building by adding headroom. Example: #251, Page 21, Wingham	
Gable: the triangular portion of a wall between the edges of a sloping roof. **Jacobean Gable:** the gable extends above the roofline. Example: Page 16, Wingham	
Hipped Roof: a roof where all sides slope downwards to the walls with no gables. Example: #133, Auburn, Page 47	
Keystones and Voussoirs: a voussoir is a wedge-shaped element used in building an arch. A keystone is the central stone that locks all the stones into position, allowing the arch to bear weight. A keystone is often enlarged and embellished. Example: Page 16, Wingham	
Lancet Window: a tall, narrow window with a pointed arch at its top. Example: Auburn Knox United Church, Page 47	

Quoin: masonry blocks at the corner of a wall, often a decorative feature, usually larger or of a different colour than the rest of the wall. Example: Blyth, Page 53	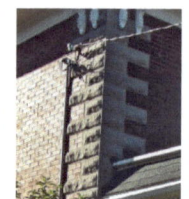
Rose Window: a circular window with ornamental tracery radiating from the centre. Example: Blyth Christian Reformed Church, Page 53	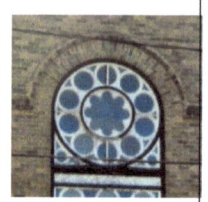
Sidelight: a vertical window that flanks a door, and is often used to emphasize the importance of a primary entrance. **Transom Window:** the light above the doorway, also called a fanlight. Example: #326, Page 39, Wingham	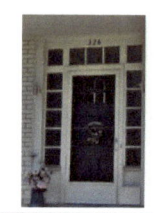
Verge board and Finial: also called bargeboards – hang from the projecting end of a roof and are often elaborately carved and ornamented. **Finial:** ornament added to the top of a gable, pinnacle, canopy or spire – a Gothic element. Example: Page 17, Wingham	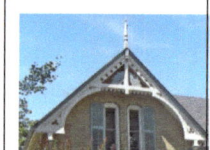

Building Styles

Edwardian, 1900-1930 – This style bridges the ornate and elaborate styles of the Victorian era and the simplified styles of the 20th century. Edwardian Classicism provided simple, balanced facades, simple rooflines, dormer windows, large front porches, and smooth brick surfaces. Voussoirs and keystones are used sparingly and are understated. Finials and cresting are absent. Cornice brackets and braces are block-like and openings have flat arches or plain stone lintels. Example: Page 17, Wingham	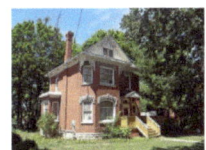
Gothic Revival, 1830-1890 – These decorative buildings have sharply-pitched gables with highly detailed verge boards, pointed-arch window openings, and dichromatic brickwork. It is a common style in Ontario. Example: 101 John Street, Page 26, Wingham	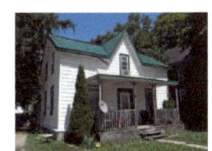
Italianate, 1850-1900 – A two story rectangular building with a mild hip roof, a projecting frontispiece, and generous eaves with ornate cornice brackets was the basis of the style; often there are large sash windows, quoins, ornate detailing on the windows, belvederes and wraparound verandahs. Italianate commercial buildings often have cast iron cresting and elegant window surrounds. Example:	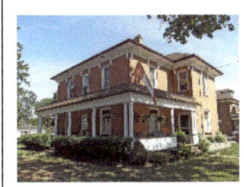

Neo-Classical, 1810-1850 – This style was a direct result of the War of 1812. Many Upper Canadians returning from the war with the United States were second or third generation Loyalists who had inherited land and means from their forefathers. Once the conflict had passed, they had the money and the time to expand their holdings and indulge their architectural whims. Both residential and commercial buildings were constructed on the traditional Georgian plan, but they had a new gaiety and light-heartedness. Detailing became more refined, delicate, and elegant.	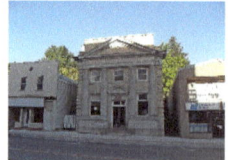
Regency Cottage, 1830-1860 – This style originated in England in 1815 and spread to Ontario later in the 19th century as British officers retired to Canada. It is a modest one-story house with a low-pitched hip roof and has a symmetrical front façade. Example: 155 Shuter Street, Page 29, Wingham	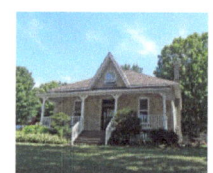

Romanesque Revival, 1880-1910 – This style hearkens back to medieval architecture of the 11th and 12th centuries with a heavy appearance, blocky towers and rounded arches. Example:	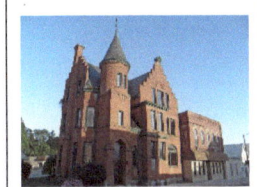
Second Empire, 1860-1880 – The mansard roof is the most noteworthy feature of this style and is evidence of the French origins. Projecting central towers and one or two-story bays can also be present. Example: 274 Josephine Street, Page 9	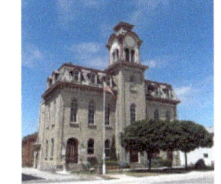

Other Books by Barbara Raue

Coins of Gold
Arrows, Indians and Love
The Life and Times of Barbara
The Cromwell Family Book
Laura Secord Discovered
Daddy Where Are You?

Montana Series
Book 1: Montana Dream
Book 2: Life on the Montana Frontier
Book 3: Montana to Boston and Back
Book 4: Montana Sons Go to War
Book 5: Montana Sons Return from War

Donaldson Series
Book 1: Rite of Passage
Book 2: Rite of Marriage

© 2022 by Barbara Raue - All the photos in this book have been taken with my cameras. I own the rights to them.

Barbara is The Authority on Saving Our History One Photo at a Time. She is pursuing her interest in photography and architecture by preserving a record through photos of old buildings from the 1800s and 1900s with their unique architecture. Enjoy the beautiful architecture in the comfort of your living room. Dream about what it was like in those by-gone days. Dream about what it was like to live in a mansion like one of those in this book.

Barbara Raue, a wife, mother and grandmother, is an avid reader and writer. She has researched and compiled several family histories. In 2010, Barbara published her book "Coins of Gold," which celebrates the courageous life of her mother, May Todd. Barbara's second book is a historical fiction "Arrows, Indians and Love" which takes place in Boonesborough, Kentucky during the time of Daniel Boone. In 2013, Barbara published *The Cromwell Family Book* in which she traces her ancestry generations back into Great Britain. Her second novel is called *Laura Secord Discovered,* in which the story of Laura's service during the War of 1812 is shared. Barbara's memoir is titled *Daddy Where Are You?* It tells of her life growing up without a father. Five novels in the Montana Series have been published, *Montana Dream, Life on the Montana Frontier, Montana to Boston and Back, Montana Sons Go to War*, and *Montana Sons Return from War*. The Donaldson series of two novels is available: *Rite of Passage* and *Rite of Marriage*.

This is a link to Barbara's website to view all of her books
http://barbararaue.ca

www.ingramcontent.com/pod-product-compliance
Lightning Source LLC
Chambersburg PA
CBHW040231220526
45473CB00001B/200